15 FLOWERS, PLANTS AND ANIMALS
FOR YOU TO PAINT

BOTANICAL WATERCOLOUR ART PAD

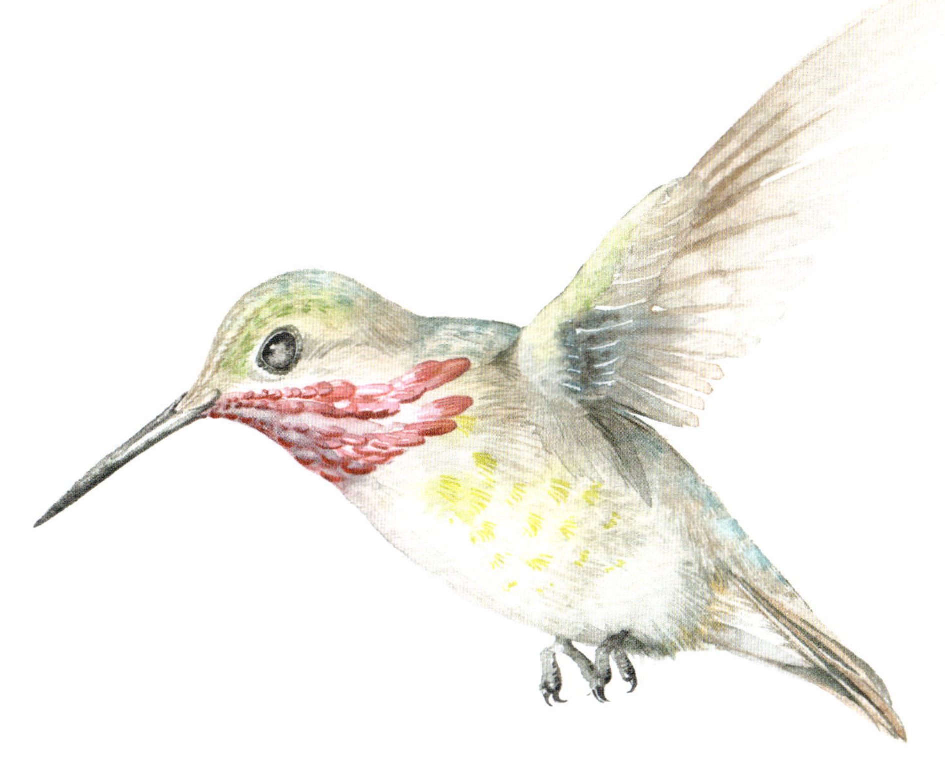

HARRIET DE WINTON

ilex

First published in Great Britain
in 2026 by Ilex, an imprint of
Octopus Publishing Group Ltd
Carmelite House
50 Victoria Embankment
London EC4Y 0DZ
www.octopusbooks.co.uk

An Hachette UK Company
www.hachette.co.uk

The authorised representative
in the EEA is Hachette Ireland,
8 Castlecourt Centre, Dublin 15,
D15 XTP3, Ireland
(email: info@hbgi.ie)

Distributed in the US by
Hachette Book Group
1290 Avenue of the Americas,
4th and 5th Floors,
New York, NY 10104

Distributed in Canada by
Canadian Manda Group
664 Annette St., Toronto, Ontario,
Canada M6S 2C8

ISBN 978-1-84601-709-4

A CIP catalogue record for this book is available from the British Library

Printed and bound in China

10 9 8 7 6 5 4 3 2 1

Publishing Director: Alison Starling
Commissioning Editor: Emma Hanson
Senior Developmental Editor:
Rachel Silverlight
Art Director: Ben Gardiner
Production: Katherine Hockley
and Caroline Alberti

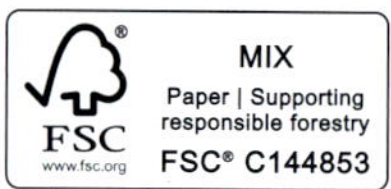

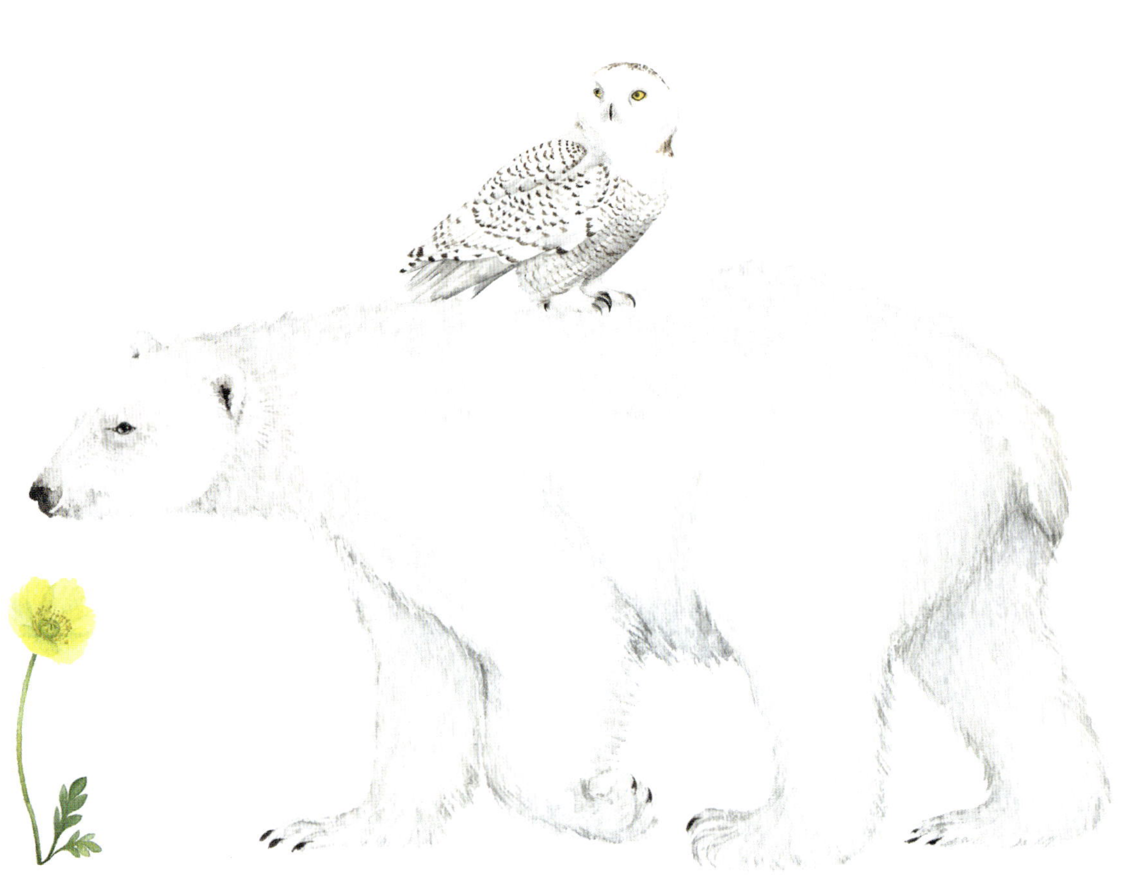

CONTENTS

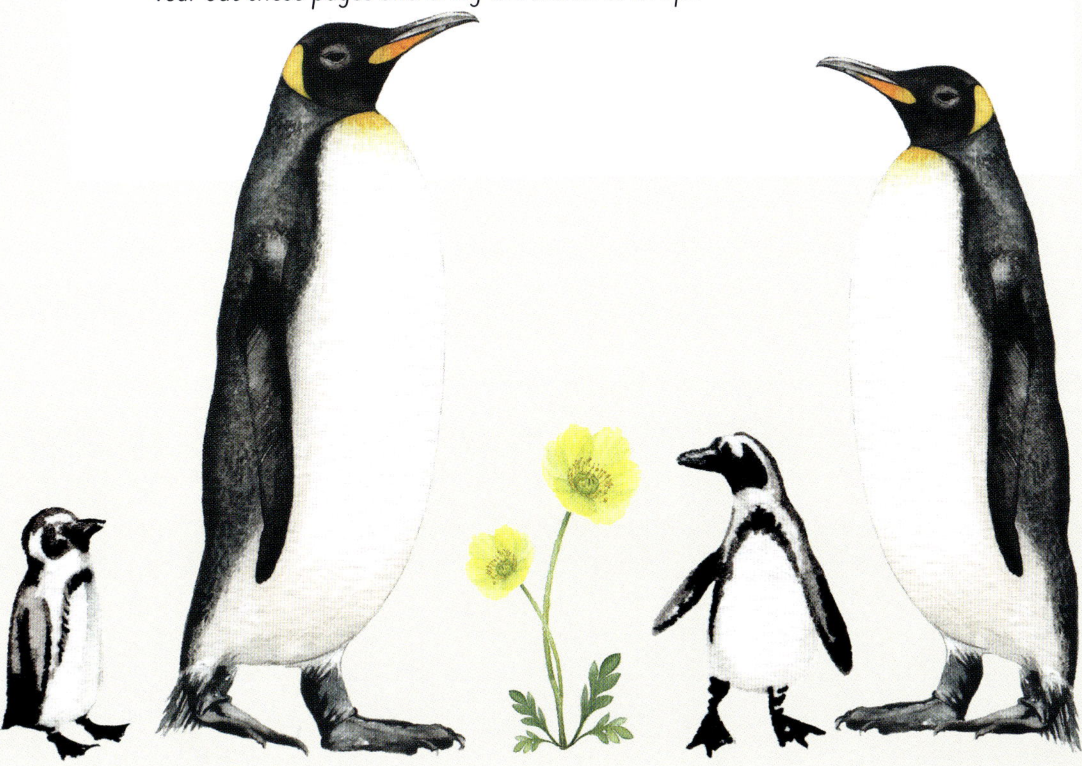

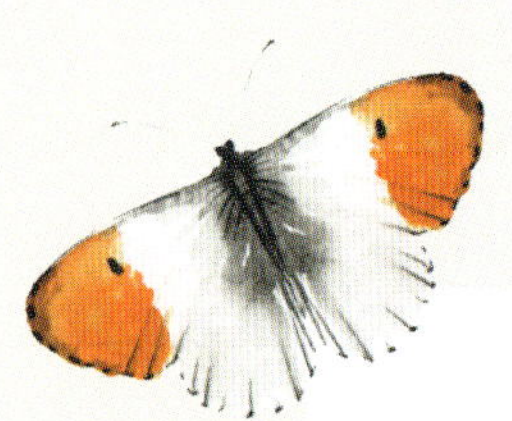

INTRODUCTION

Art is for everyone, and my goal with every book I write is to remove obstacles that stand between you and the joy of watercolour. With pages of pre-drawn pictures and patterns, you can immediately pick up a brush and play with watercolour without the worry of how to draw an accurate flamingo or zebra.

Colouring is wonderfully therapeutic, and this botanical art pad is full of simple, whimsical line drawings that offer just the right balance of detail, making them perfect for beginners or anyone looking for a stress-free creative escape. Printed on high-quality paper to handle watercolours, markers, or coloured pencils without bleeding, you can really let your imagination run wild with colour combinations and patterns.

First, check out the materials list and basic techniques to get the best out of these painting projects. As you progress through the book you can refer back to these technique guides at any time.

Travel with your paintbrush across continents and climates – this is your opportunity to dive into the world of watercolour with no drawing required.

HOW TO USE THIS BOOK

CHOOSE AN ARTWORK:

Refer to the gallery of finished artworks to select which composition you would like to paint. Then find the page with its printed outline in the art pad section in the second half of the book.

REMOVE THE PAGE:

Carefully remove the page from the book by pressing down on the opposite page and pulling firmly. In order to prevent the paper buckling from the water and paint, I suggest you secure it to a surface with masking tape before you start painting.

USE THE GALLERY AND TUTORIALS:

Refer back to the gallery if you'd like to copy the colours I have used for these artworks, or come up with your own designs. At the front of the book you will find tutorials for animal fur, insects, bird feathers and flower petals to give you the skills you need to complete any painting in this book.

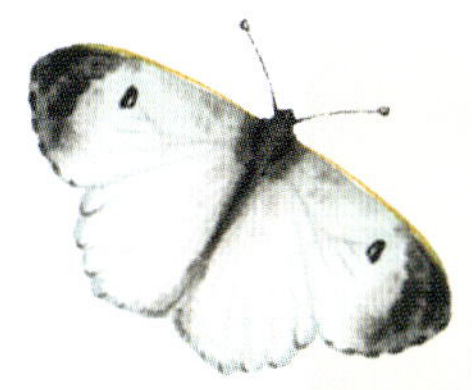

MATERIALS

Watercolour painting requires a relatively affordable and simple kit list. In buying the best quality materials within your budget and treating them with great care, you should seldom need to restock or replace.

PAINT

I use a combination of tubes and pans of watercolour; both have their advantages. Pans (dry, concentrated blocks of watercolour) come in easily transportable sets with built-in palettes. If you are likely to stick a paint-covered brush into the wrong pan, it can get a bit messy – you'd be better off using tubes of paint.

Watercolour is rather like food colouring: it is so concentrated that you only need the tiniest bit to create a vibrant colour. The better the quality of paint, the higher the percentage of pigment, resulting in a more vibrant and long-lasting colour. Brands such as Daler-Rowney and Winsor & Newton have a student range and a professional range. The student range will have more binder and less pigment than the professional range, but the standard is still fairly decent. I use professional-quality Daler-Rowney on a daily basis but other brands to look out for are Schmincke and Sennelier.

A tube of white gouache or acrylic paint is a useful addition to paint opaque highlights at the end of a piece.

BRUSHES

Pointed round brushes are brilliantly versatile: the bristles form a fine tip but are plentiful enough to create a broad line. I recommend having a range of medium sizes (0, 2, 4, 6) as well as some smaller detail brushes (4/0, 2/0). If you want to add colour to large areas or background washes, you will need a mop brush to carry large amounts of liquid.

Your brushes will last longer if you clean them thoroughly after use and never leave them bristles down in a jar of water. The paint will flake off the handle of a brush left in water, making it uncomfortable to hold, not to mention the poor bristles being bent out of shape.

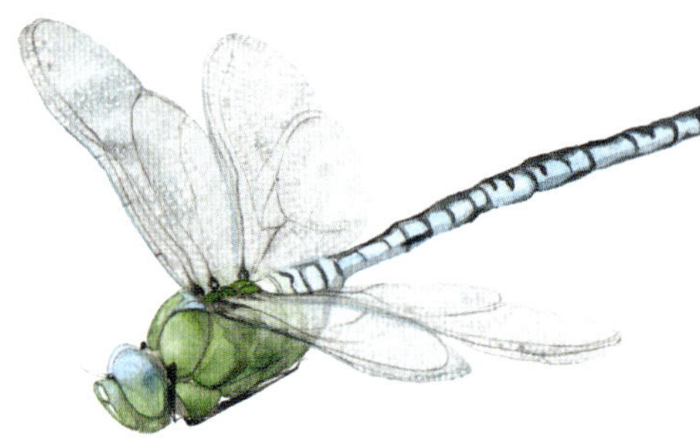

PALETTE

When using paint tubes, a ceramic plate works just fine as a palette. If you are working with plenty of wet colour, it is wise to buy a palette with wells that separate the paint. You can buy plastic, ceramic and enamel metal palettes, but I find ceramic is best for mixing watercolours (why I often end up using a plate).

WATER JAR

Any low-ball glass, mug or plastic container will do as long as its sides aren't too high. I prefer a clear vessel so I can see when to replenish the water. Painting with swamp water will inevitably affect the colours on your page. I work with two jars of water: one to clean off the brush and the other to dip the newly clean brush into.

KITCHEN PAPER

I always place my palette on the edge of a piece of kitchen paper to stop it from sliding about and also to blot my brush dry. When blotting it like this you will find hidden paint lingering in the seemingly clean bristles, warranting another swish in the water.

PAPER

It's always a good idea to have some spare sheets of watercolour paper to practise the basic techniques before getting started in this book.

YOUR WORKSPACE

Seat yourself at a table in a space with as much natural light as possible. Feeling good in your environment both mentally and physically is so important when it comes to being creative.

WATERCOLOUR BASICS: PAINTING TECHNIQUES

These painting techniques will help you explore the two vital components – water and colour – and how much of each to use. Adding different amounts of water to the paint in your palette will change the consistency and the colour. Dilute it to a light, transparent tone that easily flows across the page, or use the bare minimum of water to make a thick and heavy colour with a rich intensity.

PAINTING TECHNIQUES

Watercolour pigment is intensely concentrated – you only need the tiniest bit. Water is the vehicle for the colour to travel, and it does most of the work. The golden rule of watercolour is your brush should always be wet. I don't mean waterlogged at all times, but the bristles need to be damp enough to hold paint even when working on precise detail. Swish the brush around in your water jar and wipe the bristles on the rim a few times. This allows paint to flow from brush to page as smoothly as a felt-tip pen. Throughout this book I will refer to the paint as wet, diluted and concentrated.

Wet: plenty of water on the brush with plenty of colour, allowing for broad coverage and bright, seamless blending.

Diluted: plenty of water and very little colour to achieve a pale, translucent quality.

Concentrated: used most often for precise detail in the final stages of a painting; a good coverage of colour on the brush with minimal water.

The following painting techniques are all carried out with a size 4 pointed round brush.

Dry on dry

Applying concentrated paint to a dry surface: either a dry page or a painted page that has dried fully.

Your brush should never be bone dry, otherwise the paint will be applied in a dry-brushed manner.

Painting a concentrated circle on a dry page will not lead to anything very exciting, but the colour will be opaque and won't run on the dry page.

Wet on dry

Applying wet paint to a dry surface: either a dry page or a painted page that has dried fully.

Clean your brush off and wet it again. Fill in that dry-on-dry circle with water, stroking the brush to pick up colour from the inner edge of the circle, and watch the colour blend inwards. An initial sweep round will bring in a paler colour to fill the circle. A few more strokes will intensify the colour to make a solid colour circle. The outer edge of the circle is still crisp on the dry paper.

Alternatively, painting a new circle in a more diluted colour will result in an even, translucent shape.

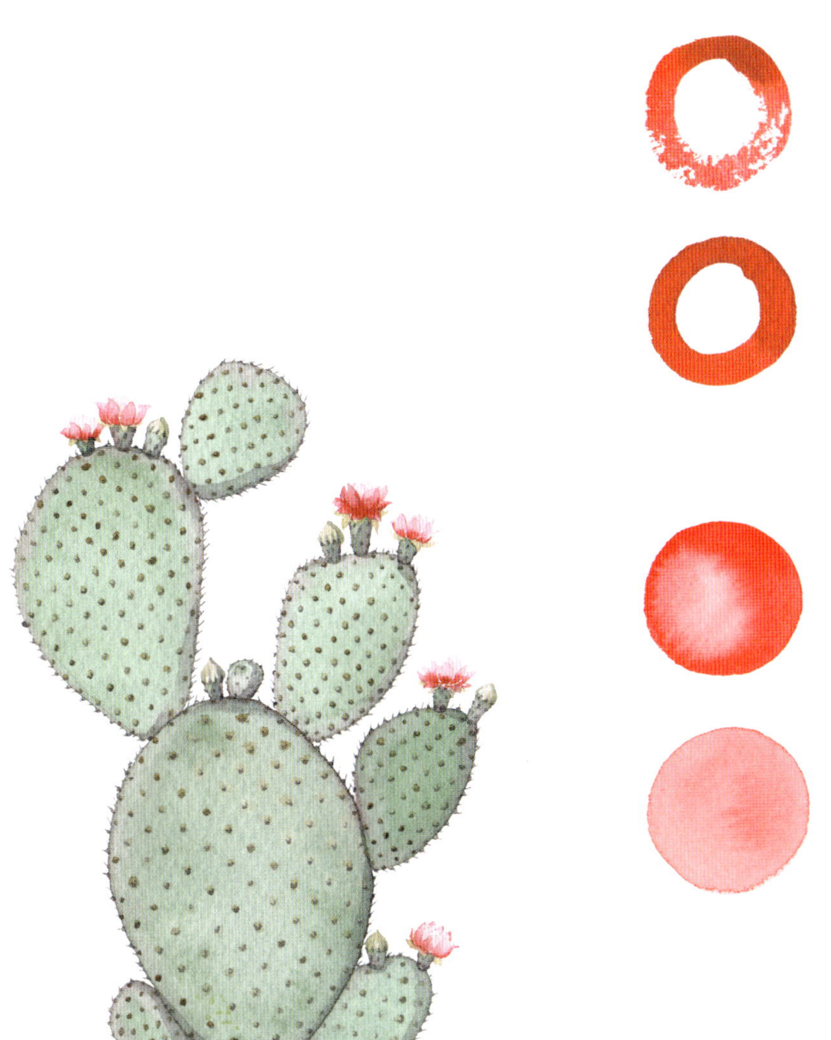

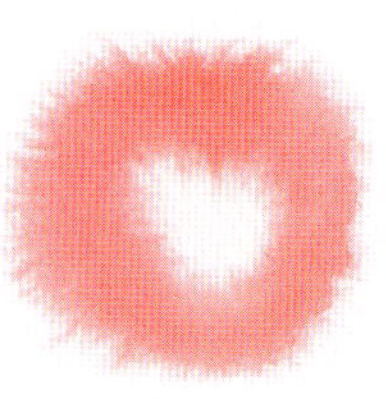

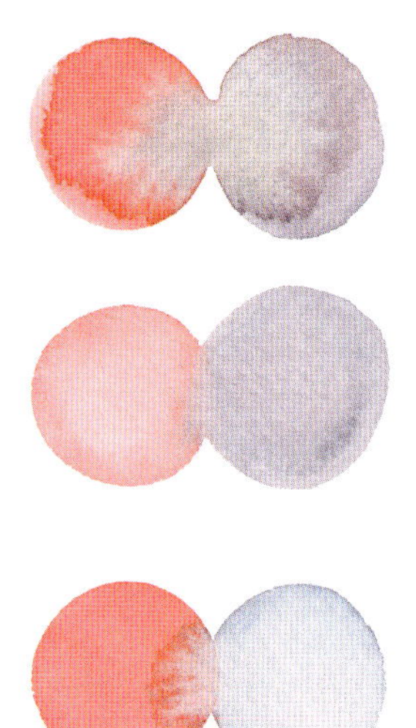

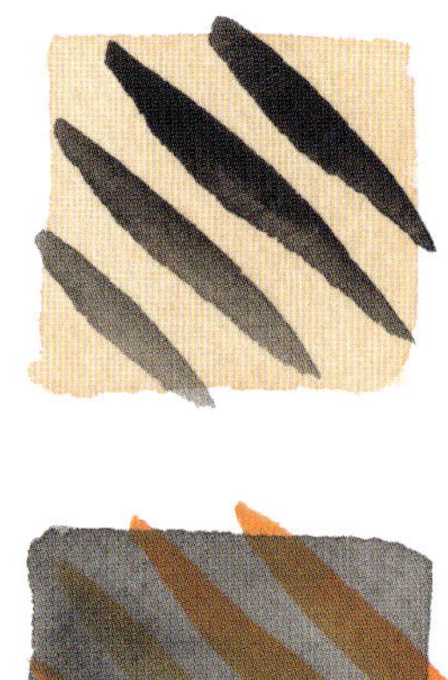

Wet on wet
Applying wet paint to a wet surface when you want to create a soft, diffused edge and a seamless blend.

With a clean brush, wet a section of page (don't leave puddles of standing water but just make the surface evenly damp), approximately 5cm (2in) square. Paint that same red circle with your wet brush and watch the paint feather out. The more you soak your page, the more unruly your watercolour will be in its travels. It is tempting to prod and poke the watercolour tendrils, but this technique is always more effective when you let the paint do its thing, undisturbed.

Standing water vs an even blend
If you are left with puddles of standing water having wet your page, you've gone too far. Colour that is applied to puddles struggles to reach the page and results in an uncontrollable and erratic blend. It can be saved by gently blotting your puddles with kitchen paper. A piece of paper that has been wetted evenly with no puddles allows for smooth and even blends.

Blending
When working on a composition, you add colour either by blending (wet on wet) or layering (wet on dry, dry on dry). Blending colours involves a little restraint.

Paint a wet circle, then choose a different wet colour and paint a second, just overlapping the circle. As long as you are using enough water in your colour mix the paint will do its thing unaided.

Refrain from prodding the two colours into each other with your brush. This can lead to over-mixing, which nearly always results in a dull, flat colour.

Try to balance the wetness of each shape. If one colour holds more water than the other, you will get this bloom effect.

Layering
Once a layer of paint is bone dry, you can add additional layers of colour and detail with no fear of it bleeding.

It is far easier to add a darker or more concentrated colour to a lighter or more diluted one than the other way around. In the tutorials, I will always start with a light wash and build it up in intensity, layer by layer. Keep this in mind when you're choosing which colours to paint first.

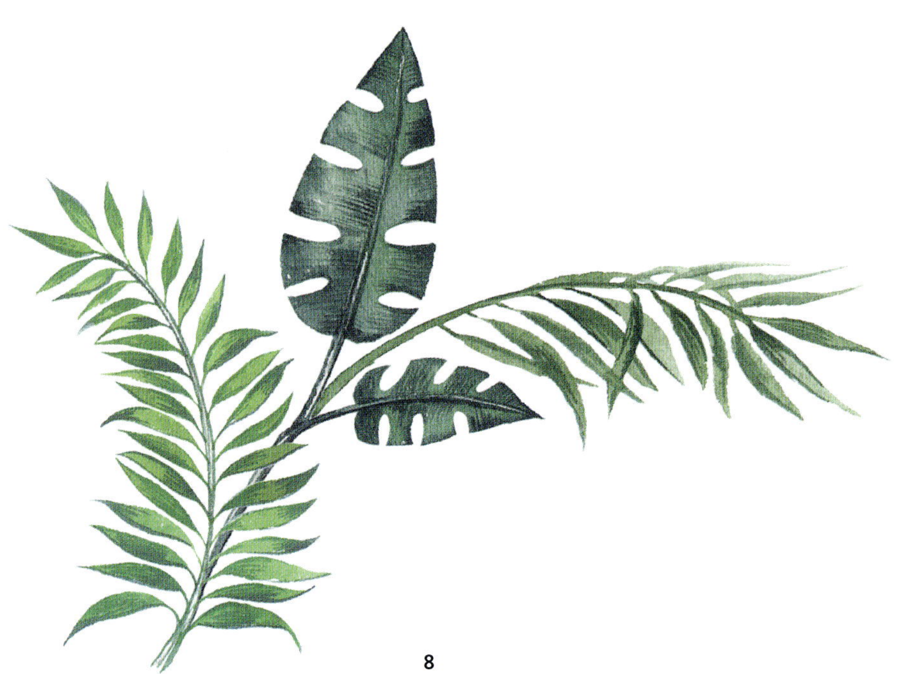

COLOUR: VALUE AND MIXING

COLOUR VALUE SCALE

'Value' is defined as the relative lightness or darkness of a colour. We use water to dilute and lighten colours, you can see this progression from light to dark in each segment of the colour wheel.

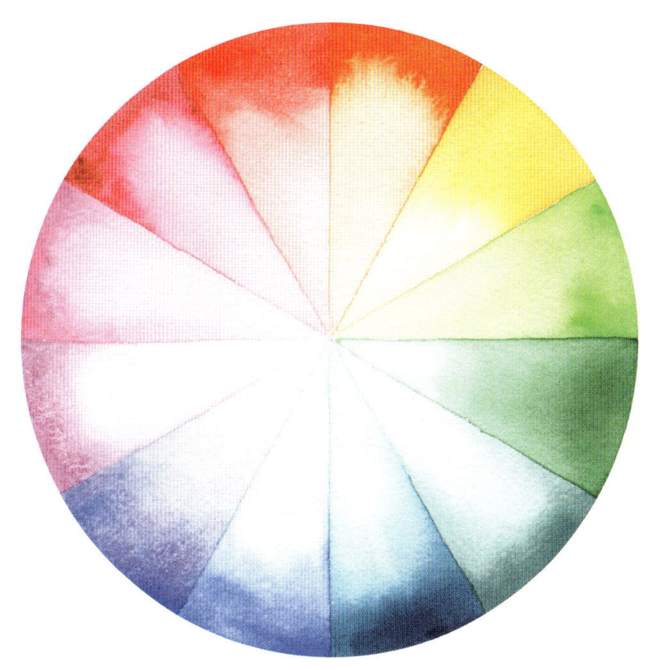

Paint a filled-in wet circle of colour. Clean your brush off and paint a filled-in circle of water that just kisses the edge of that first circle. Watch the paint burst into the wet space. Load up your brush with more water and paint another overlapped circle until you have a gradually fading caterpillar. The number of circles you achieve all depends on the amount of pigment in the first circle, the amount of water being used, and the speed at which you work. Experiment with different colours to see how they behave.

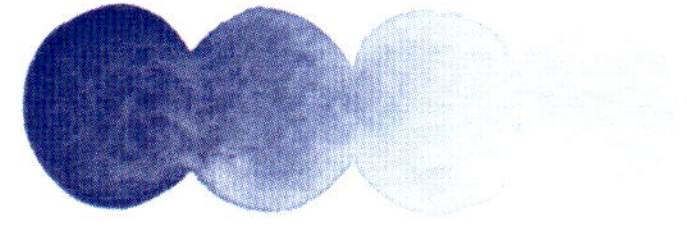

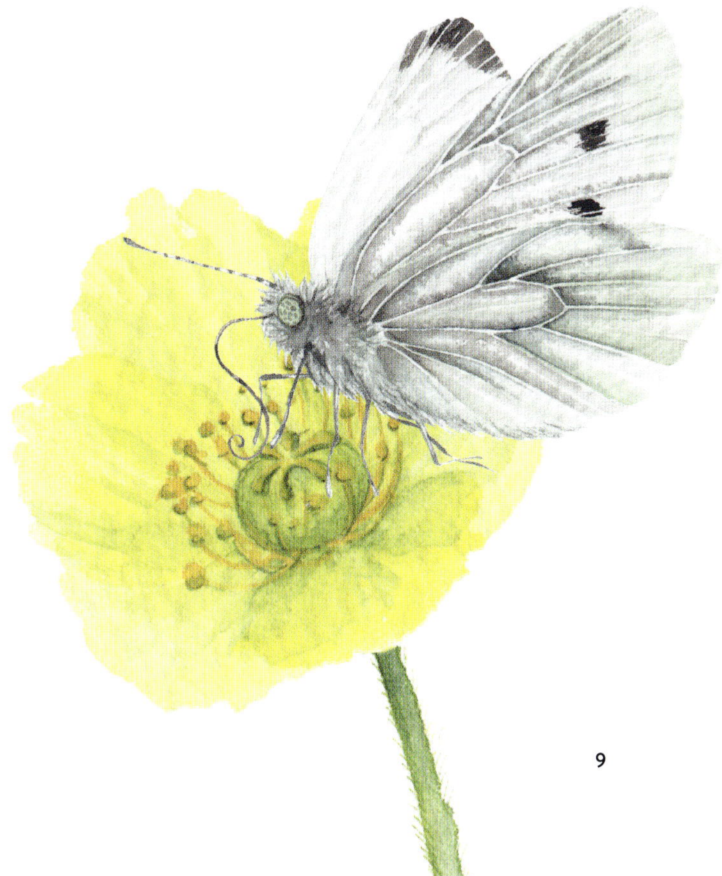

BASICS OF COLOUR MIXING

1. Use a large brush when mixing colours – it will speed up the process and give you larger quantities.
2. Make sure both colours have been woken up with water and are the same consistency.
3. Incorporate a tiny amount of the darker (or more dominant) colour into the other and you will immediately see the impact.
4. Patiently add tiny amounts of the dominant colour, fully incorporating it as you go until you achieve the colour you want.

TUTORIAL: HOW TO PAINT ANIMAL FUR

With many furry animals throughout the book, this tutorial will help you achieve a lifelike textured coat for all types of species.

1

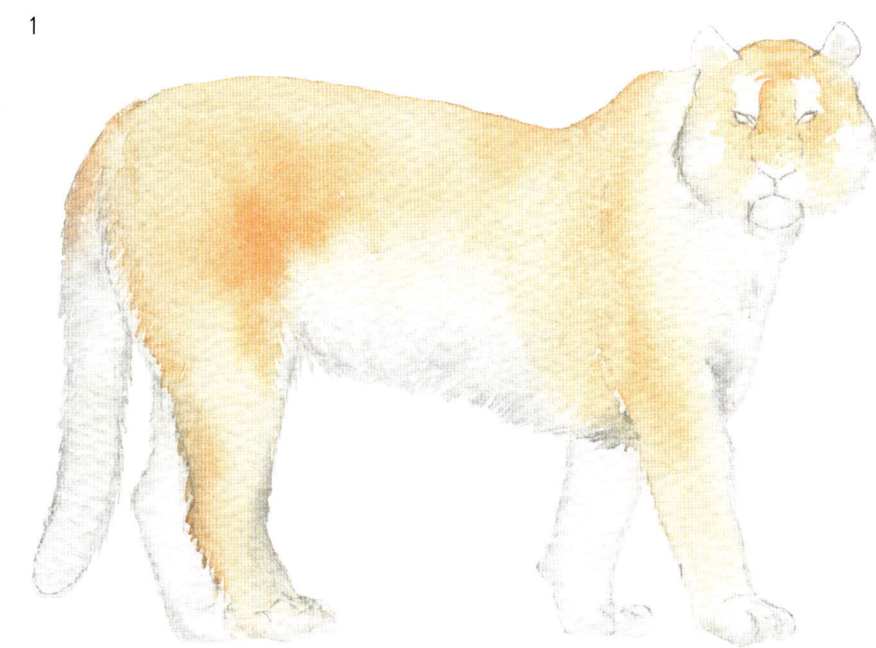

Colours

 French ultramarine blue

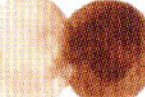 Burnt sienna

 Cadmium orange

 Yellow ochre

 Cadmium red

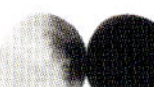 Mars black

Mixes

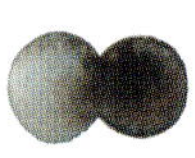 **Shadow mix:** French ultramarine blue and burnt sienna

 **Fur wash mix:** cadmium orange and yellow ochre

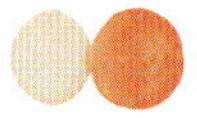 **Fur detail mix:** cadmium orange, cadmium red and burnt sienna

1.

Mix an extremely diluted shadow mix (almost transparent grey) and paint dashes with your size 0 brush along the underbelly, tail, legs and around the bottom half of the face. Blend these dashes up into the body. While still wet, use the size 4 brush to paint a wash of fur wash mix over the rest of the body, fading and blending into the shadow mix. Allow to fully dry.

2.

With your size 4/0 brush, paint fine line dashes of fur across the body in fur detail mix. Be careful to angle the dashes to the contours of the body. Add some burnt sienna dashes to the crevices behind the shoulder and by the hip.

2

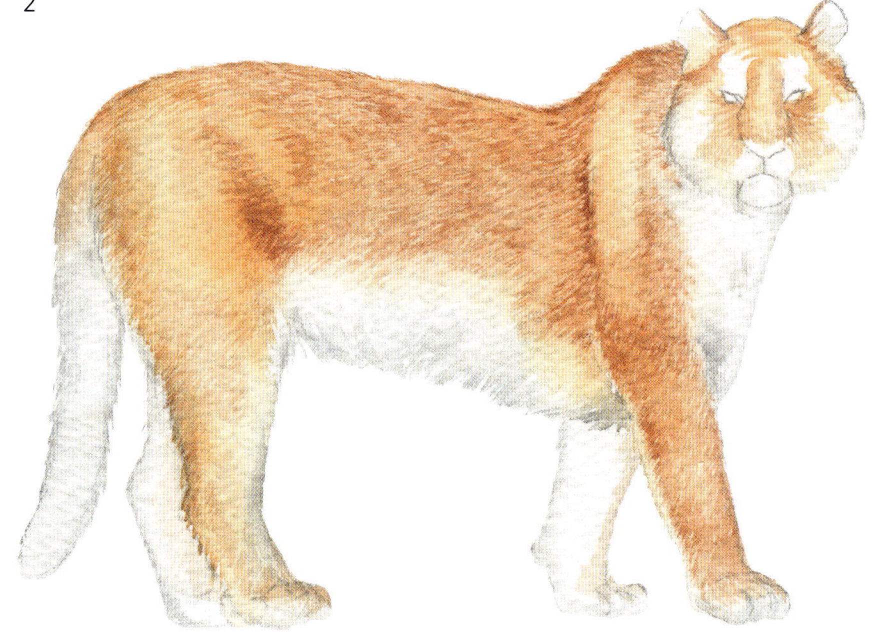

3

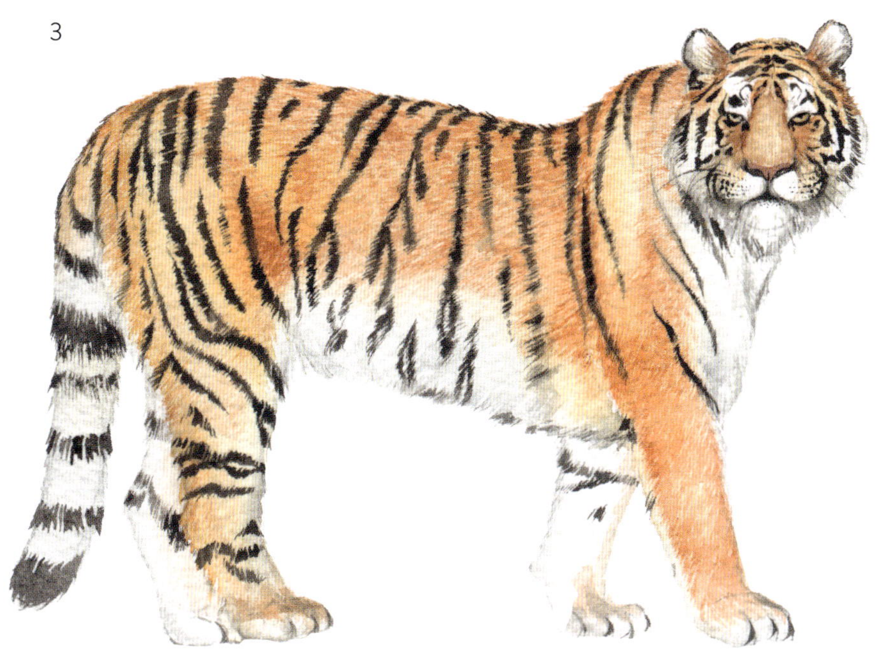

3.

Still using the size 4/0 brush, paint the eyes yellow ochre. Add burnt sienna fine lines around the temples, ears and nose. While they dry, cover the body in concentrated Mars black stripes. Create the stripes by painting strips of fine line dashes with your smallest brush. Make sure the dashes follow the angle of the fur beneath. Once the face has dried, add stripes and whiskers. Outline the eyes and dot the pupil. Add C-curve claws to the paws, all in Mars black with your smallest brush. Allow to fully dry. Rub out any visible pencil.

4.

Once dry, use the size 0 brush to paint in diluted shadow mix to any areas that require shadow.

4

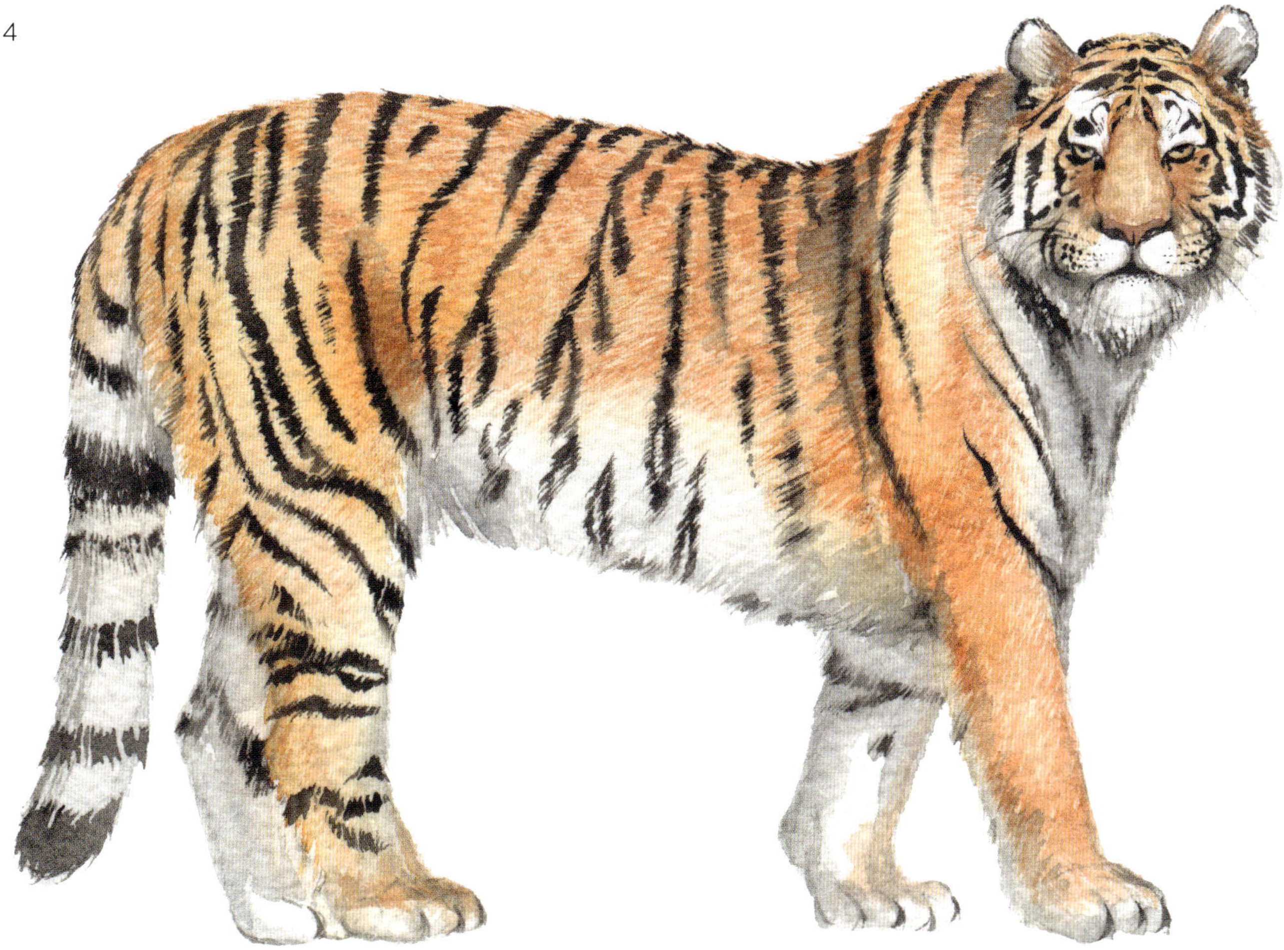

TUTORIAL: HOW TO PAINT INSECTS

Insects are nature's jewels, ornamented with intricate patterns and shiny surfaces. Achieve this richness by using contrast: pair the high shine of negative (unpainted) space with rich, concentrated colours, just like this beetle's shell.

Colours

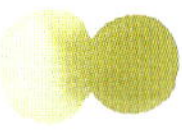 Green gold

 Hookers green

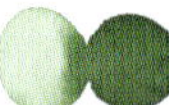 Sap green

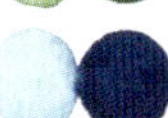 Prussian blue

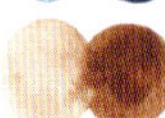 Burnt sienna

Mixes

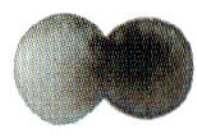 **Shadow mix:** burnt sienna and Prussian blue

1

2

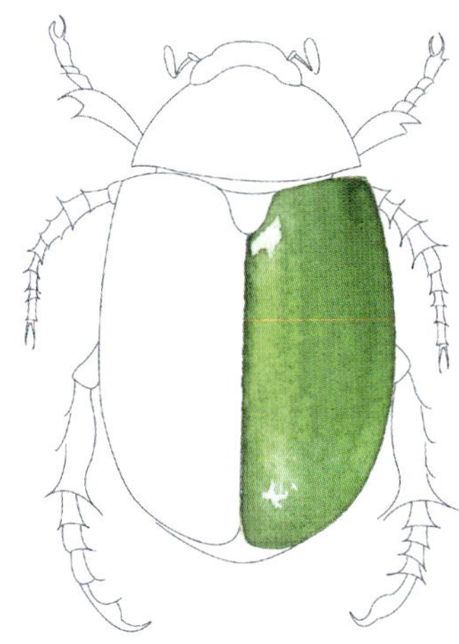

1

With a damp size 4 brush, wet one wing cover section. Paint the edges in green gold, clean the brush and use the wet bristles to draw the colour in, leaving lighter sections towards the top and bottom of the shape.

2

While still damp, using the size 4 brush, paint vertical stripes of hookers green following the curve of the shape. They will largely blend in but faint lines will still remain visible. Add a little sap green around the edges to darken the outline of the shape further.

3

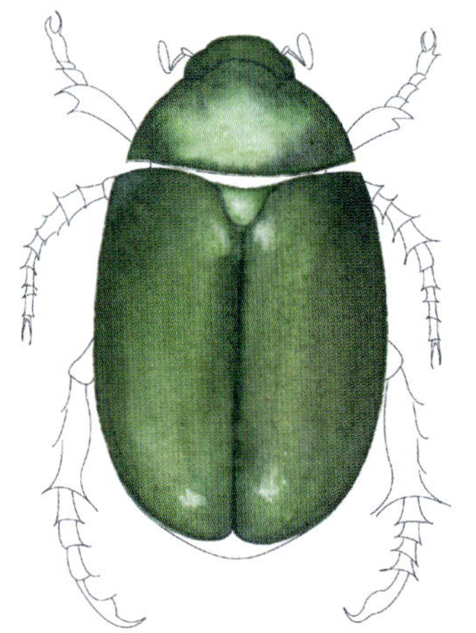

3

While still damp, use the size 4 brush to paint an outline of diluted Prussian blue. Repeat the previous steps for the other wing cover, the body and head making sure the neighbouring shape has dried before painting the new shape.

4

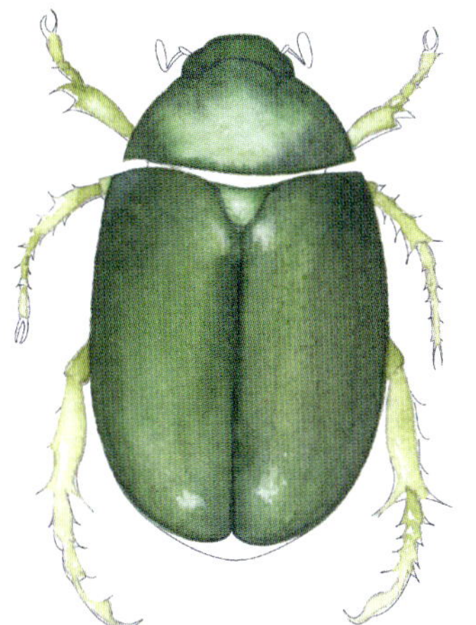

4

Paint the legs in green gold with your size 2/0 brush. Allow to dry.

5

Outline the pencil lines on the legs with hookers green followed by Prussian blue and blend inwards. Allow to dry. With your 2/0 brush, paint the fine hairs at each leg section, the antennae, below the wing coverts and neck section in shadow mix. Allow to dry and rub out any visible pencil.

5

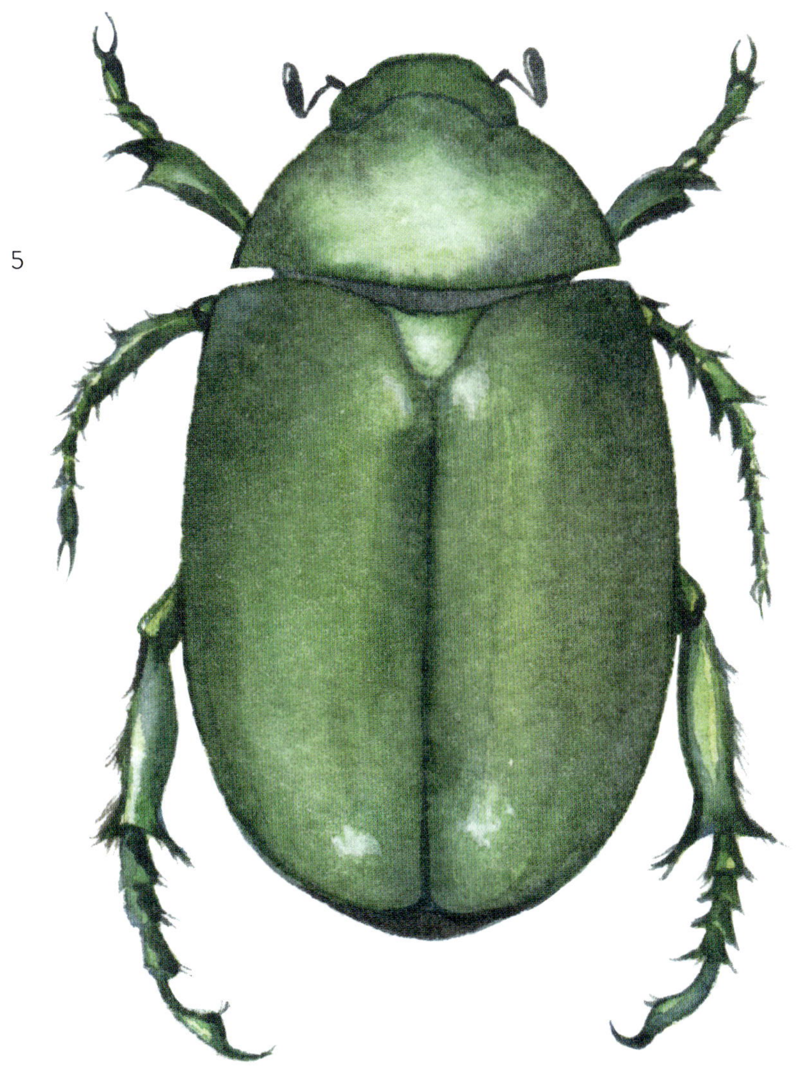

TUTORIAL: HOW TO PAINT BIRD FEATHERS

Finely detailed feathers are a perfect finishing touch to elevate your bird paintings. Use your smallest brushes to create the most delicate lines.

Colours

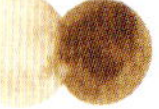 Burnt sienna

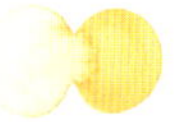 Raw umber

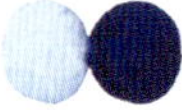 Cadmium yellow

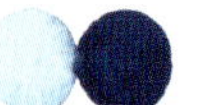 French ultramarine blue

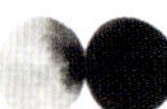 Prussian blue

 Mars black

Cadmium red

Mixes

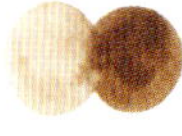 **Feather mix:** burnt sienna and raw umber

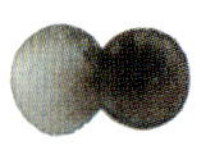 **Shadow mix:** burnt sienna and French ultramarine blue

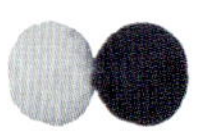 **Dark mix:** Prussian blue and Mars black

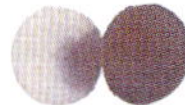 **Claw mix:** cadmium red and Prussian blue

1

2

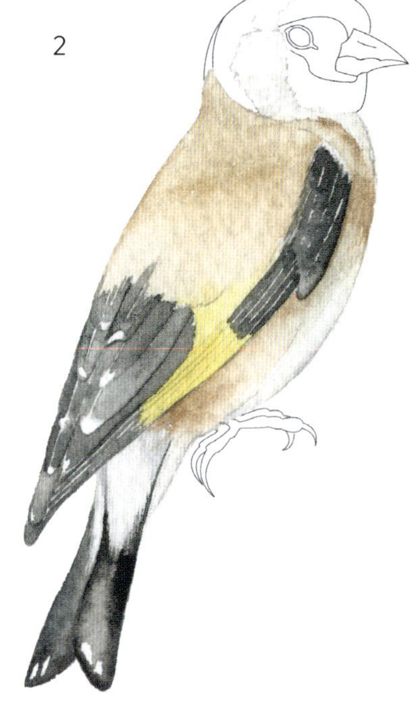

1

With your size 4 brush, paint a diluted feather mix wash across the back and torso, blend into cadmium yellow feathers halfway down the wing, and an extremely diluted shadow mix across the breast, nape, undertail coverts and tail feathers.

2

With your size 0 brush, paint the black feathers with a wash of dark mix, leaving unpainted slivers between the wing feathers and the white feather tips on the wing and tail feathers.

3

With your size 4/0 brush, paint cadmium red dashes radiating from around the beak across the front of the face. Fill in around the eye and up the back of the head with dark mix dashes. Make sure that you angle your dashes sweeping away from the beak and down the body. Fill in the beak with very diluted claw mix. The claws are painted by outlining the pencil line with claw mix and drawing the colour down into the feet with a clean wet brush. Leaving unpainted sections along the feet creates a gnarly finish.

3

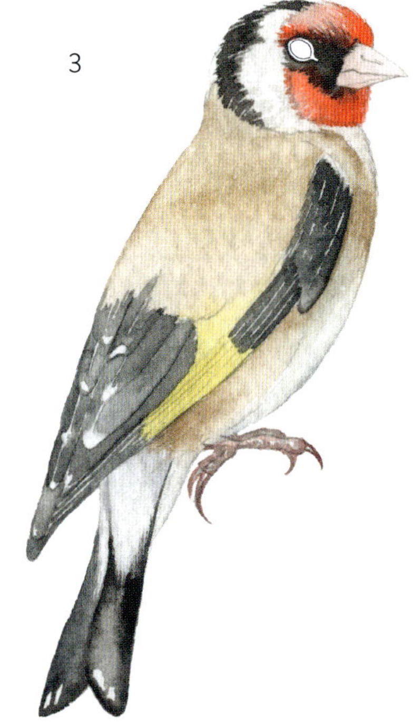

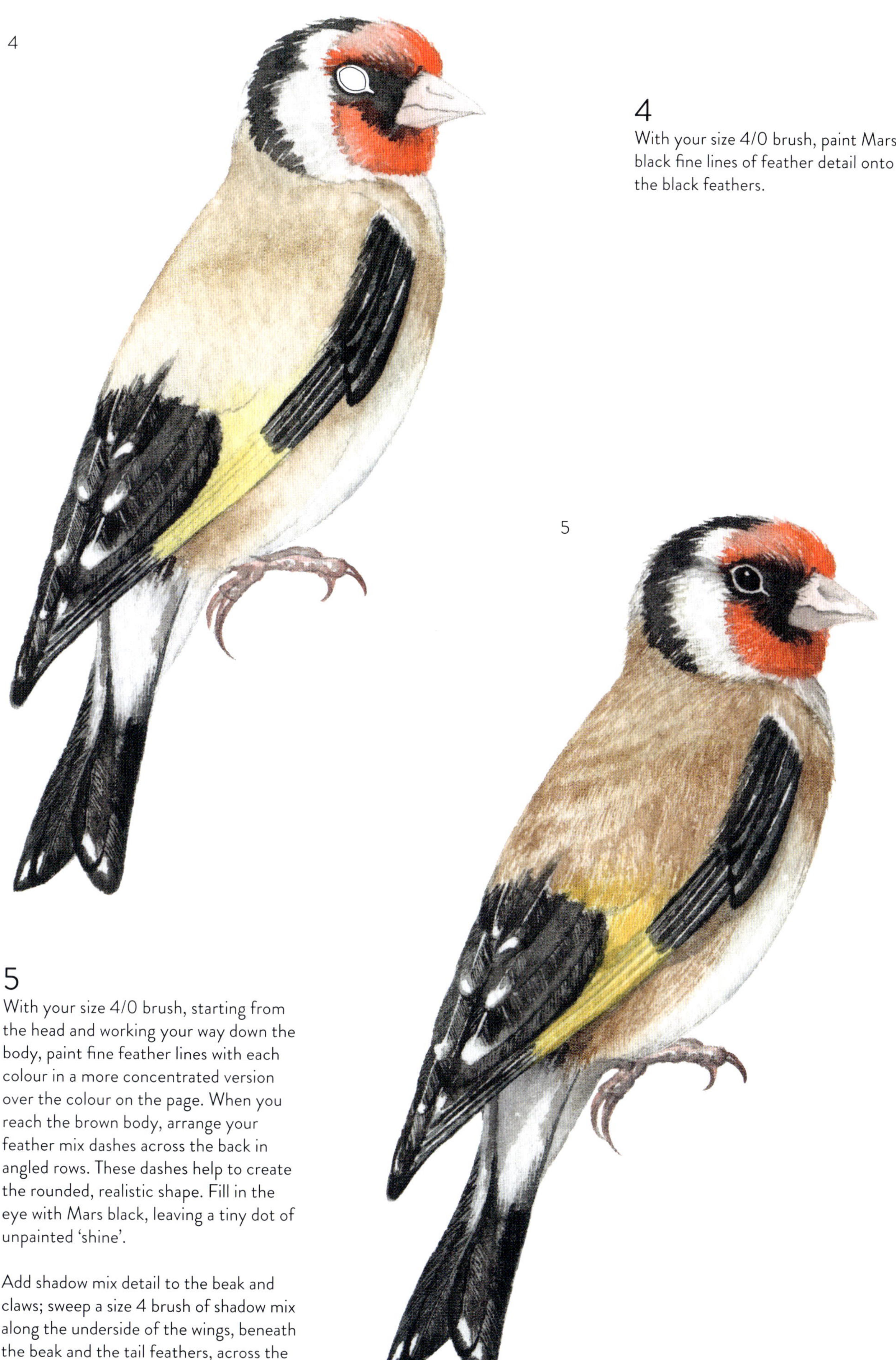

4

4

With your size 4/0 brush, paint Mars black fine lines of feather detail onto the black feathers.

5

5

With your size 4/0 brush, starting from the head and working your way down the body, paint fine feather lines with each colour in a more concentrated version over the colour on the page. When you reach the brown body, arrange your feather mix dashes across the back in angled rows. These dashes help to create the rounded, realistic shape. Fill in the eye with Mars black, leaving a tiny dot of unpainted 'shine'.

Add shadow mix detail to the beak and claws; sweep a size 4 brush of shadow mix along the underside of the wings, beneath the beak and the tail feathers, across the head and behind the eye.

TUTORIAL: HOW TO PAINT FLOWER PETALS

Petals display a range of blended, delicate colours. Remember to dilute your colours to achieve those translucent shades and crisp edges, and use as large a brush as you are comfortable with.

1

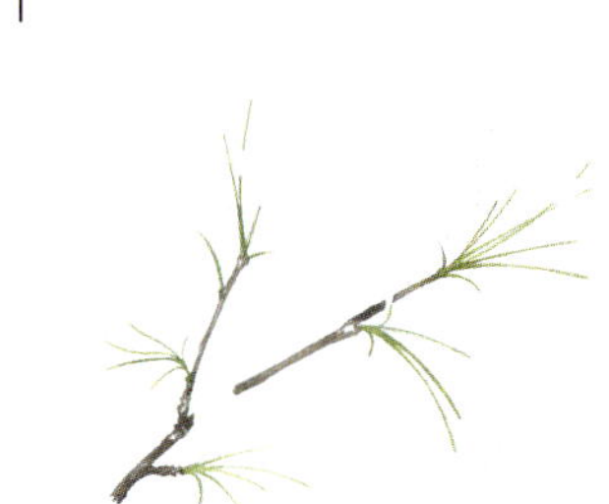

2

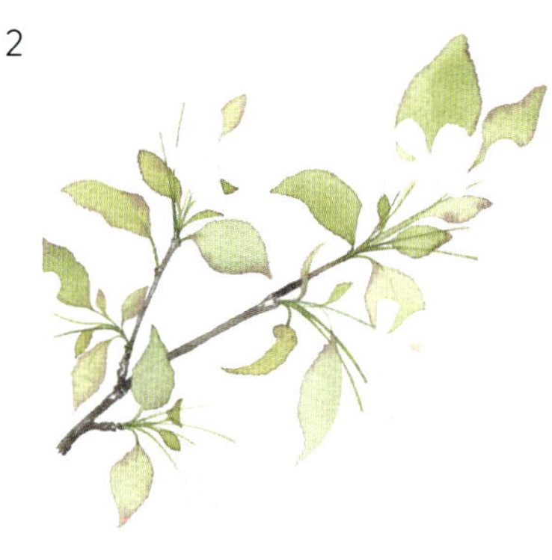

1

With your size 2 brush, paint a concentrated shadow mix branch, leaving gaps where any leaves or flowers might overlap. With your size 2/0 brush, paint using stem mix for the stems that lead to leaves, open flowers and a handful of buds.

2

Paint the leaves in diluted stem mix with your size 4 brush. While still wet, paint a jagged edge of bud mix around each leaf with your size 2/0 brush, allowing the pink colour to blend into the leaf edges. Allow to fully dry.

Colours

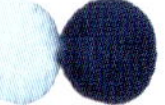 Burnt sienna

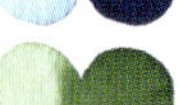 Prussian blue

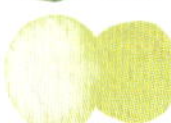 Sap green

 Green gold

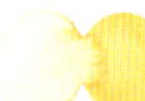 Permanent rose

 Cadmium yellow

Mars black

Mixes

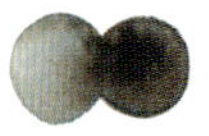 **Shadow mix:** burnt sienna and Prussian blue

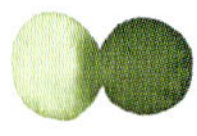 **Stem mix:** sap green and green gold

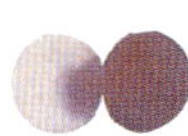 **Bud mix:** permanent rose, burnt sienna and Prussian blue

 **Petal mix:** green gold, burnt sienna and Prussian blue (all colours extremely diluted, so almost transparent)

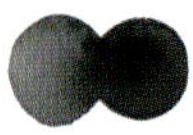 **Dark stem mix:** sap green, burnt sienna, Prussian blue and Mars black

3

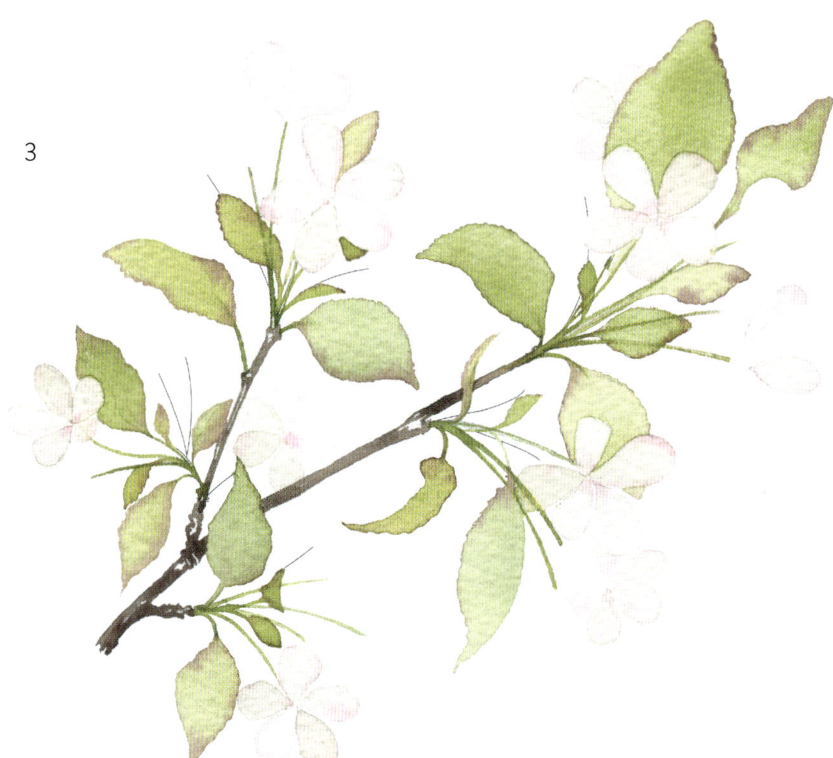

3

With your size 2 brush, paint wet petal mix flowers (five spaced-out rounded petals for each open flower and two or three for semi-open buds). While still damp, add a dab of diluted permanent rose to the petals' edges at varying places, to introduce a delicate pink tone. Allow to fully dry.

4

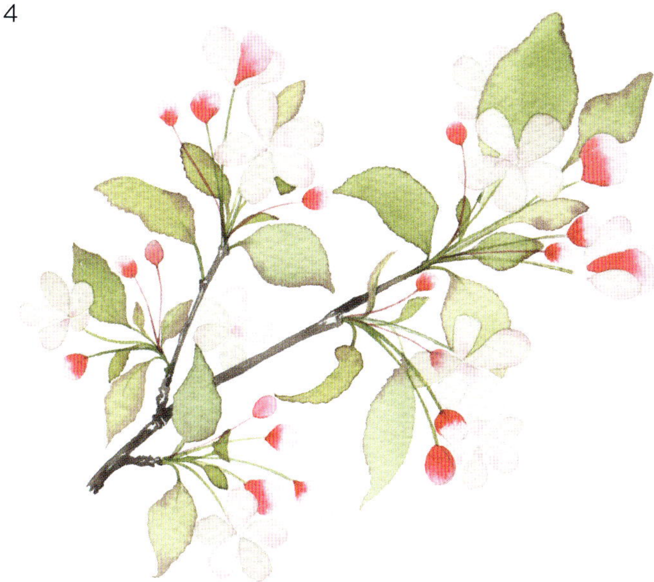

5

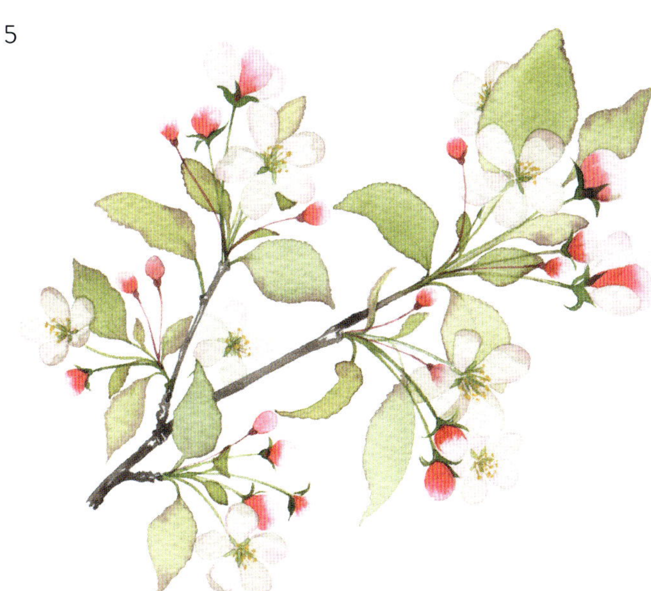

6

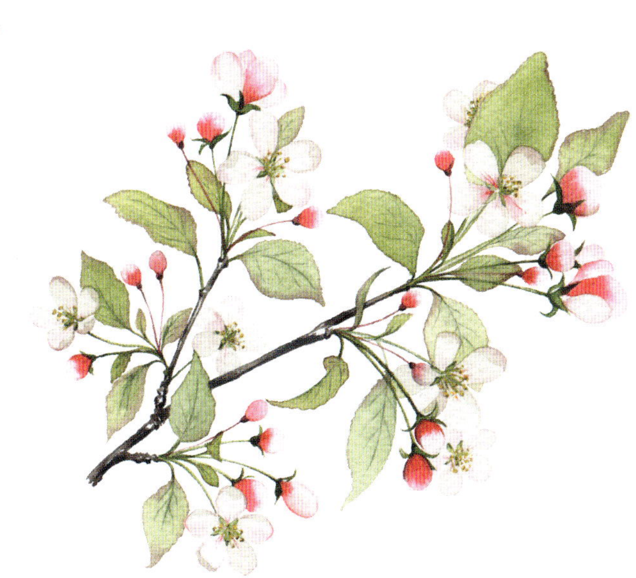

4

Paint concentrated bud mix stems up along the remaining unpainted stem lines with your size 2/0 brush. With your size 2 brush, top each empty stem (and partially painted opening bud) with a pale petal mix oval, then pulse a dab of concentrated permanent rose at the base. The pulsing motion encourages the colour to travel into the wet bud without disturbing the blend.

5

In the centre of each open flower, paint small stem mix leaves in between each petal with your size 4/0 brush. Allow to dry, then with the same brush and colour, paint fine line filaments radiating from the flower's centre (check the angle of the flower stem – your filaments will follow in that general direction). Once dry, add concentrated cadmium yellow tips to the filaments. Add a tiny dash of permanent rose to your diluted petal mix and paint C-curves on the edge of selected petals to give the impression of the curled underside of the petal. Add sap green sepals to the green-stemmed buds by painting S- and C-curves below the base of the bud. For the pink-stemmed buds, simply paint a splodge of bud mix underneath the bud.

6

With your size 4/0 brush, paint a thin line of dark stem mix from the base of the leaf centre, up the middle until it fades out. Then paint a few leaf veins, allowing them also to fade out before reaching the edge of the leaf. Allow to dry. Then with your clean and wet size 4 brush, stroke the bristles over the leaf to soften these lines. With your size 4/0 brush, use the dark stem mix to outline some of the open flower and bud sepals. Add a little Mars black to your shadow mix and add lines of detail to the branch with your size 2/0 brush.

GALLERY OF FINISHED IMAGES

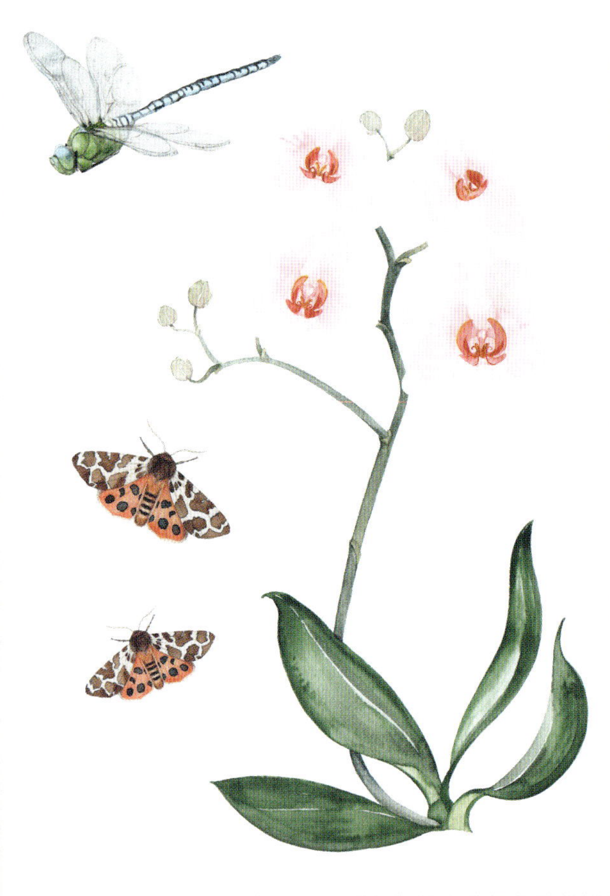

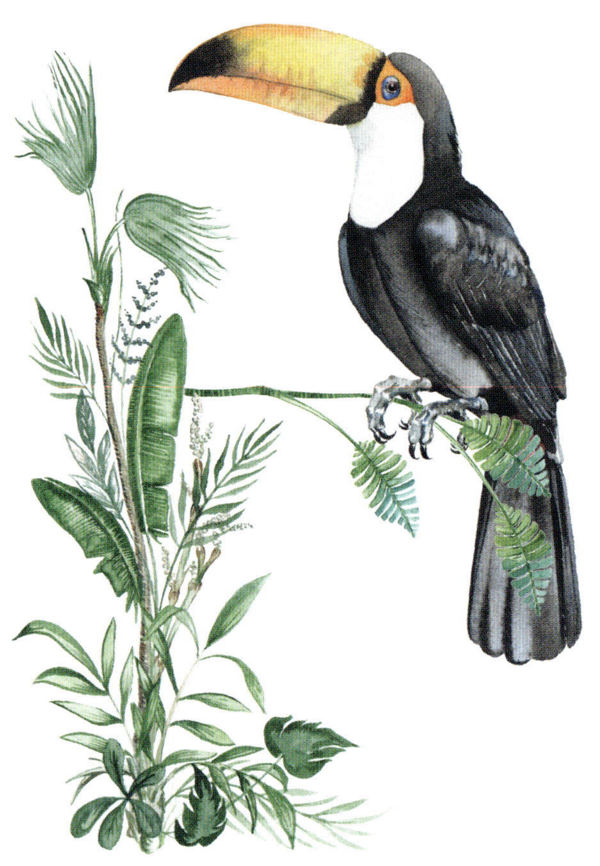

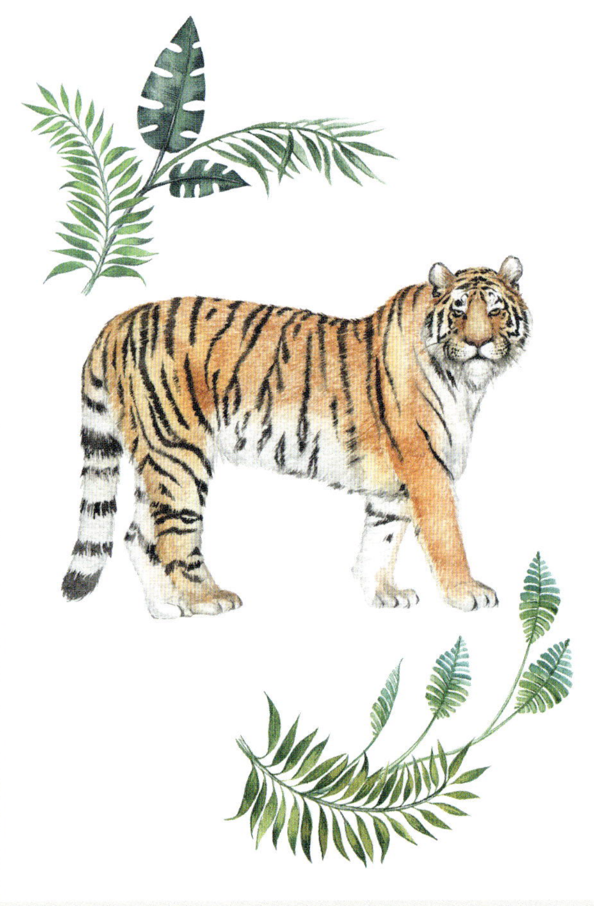

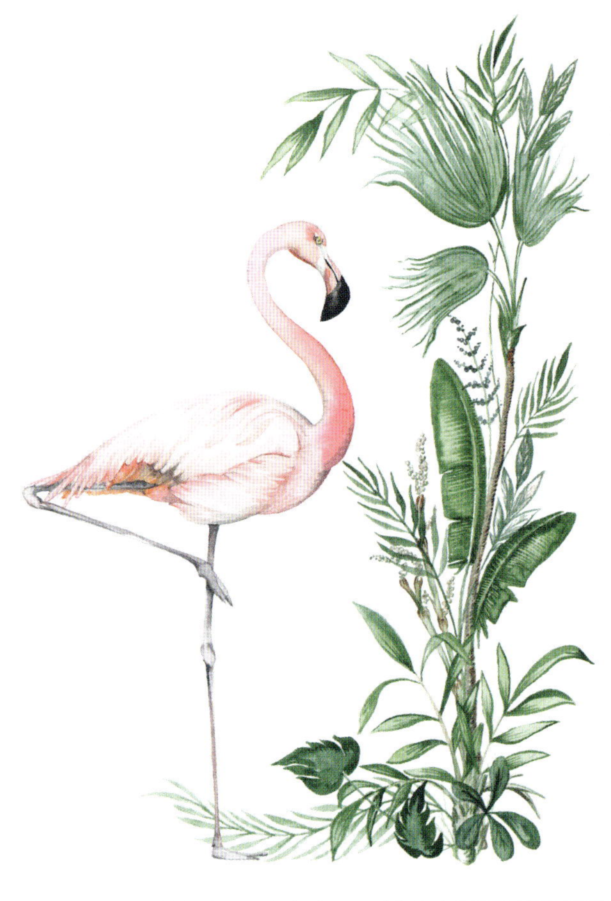

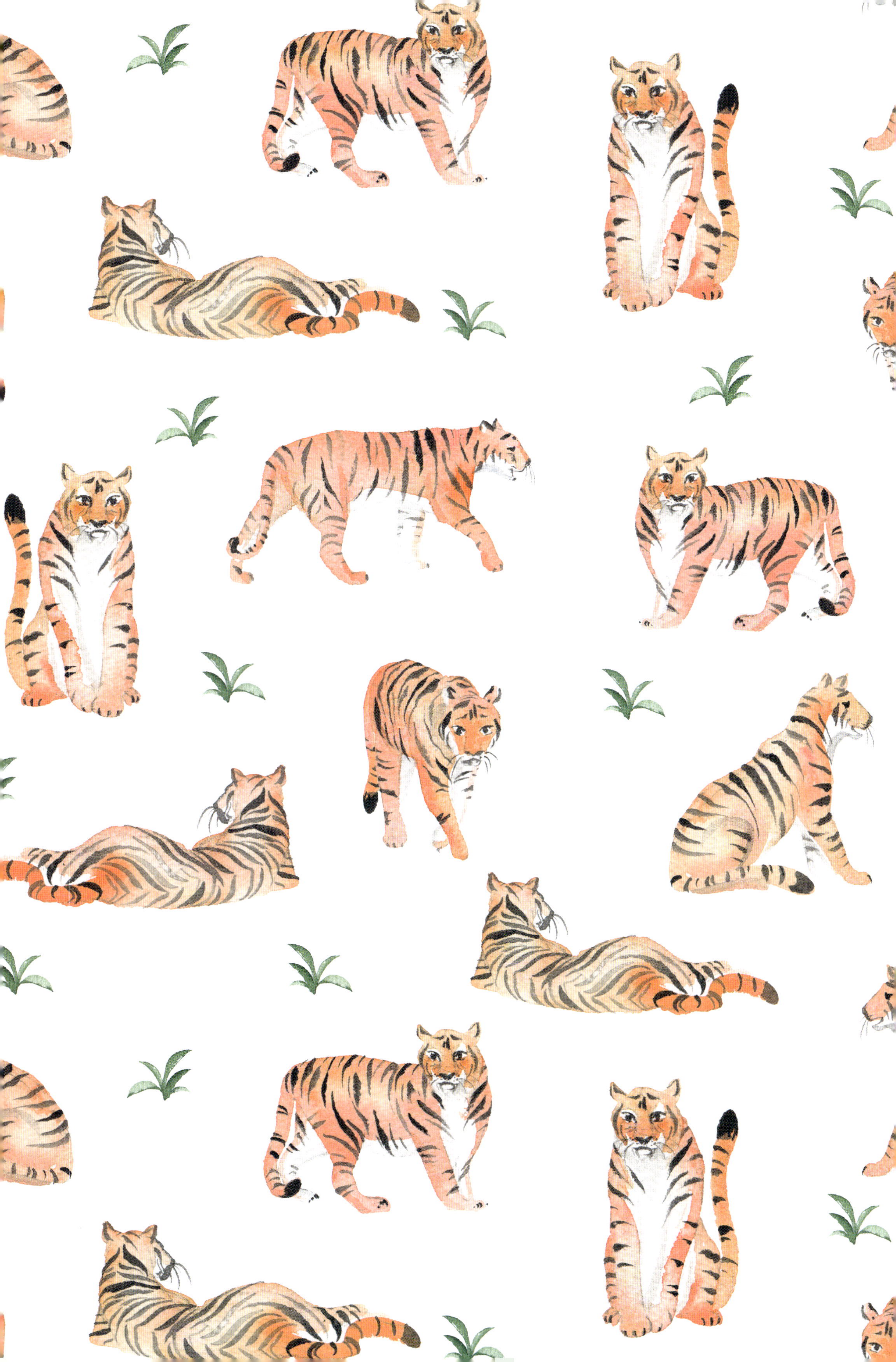

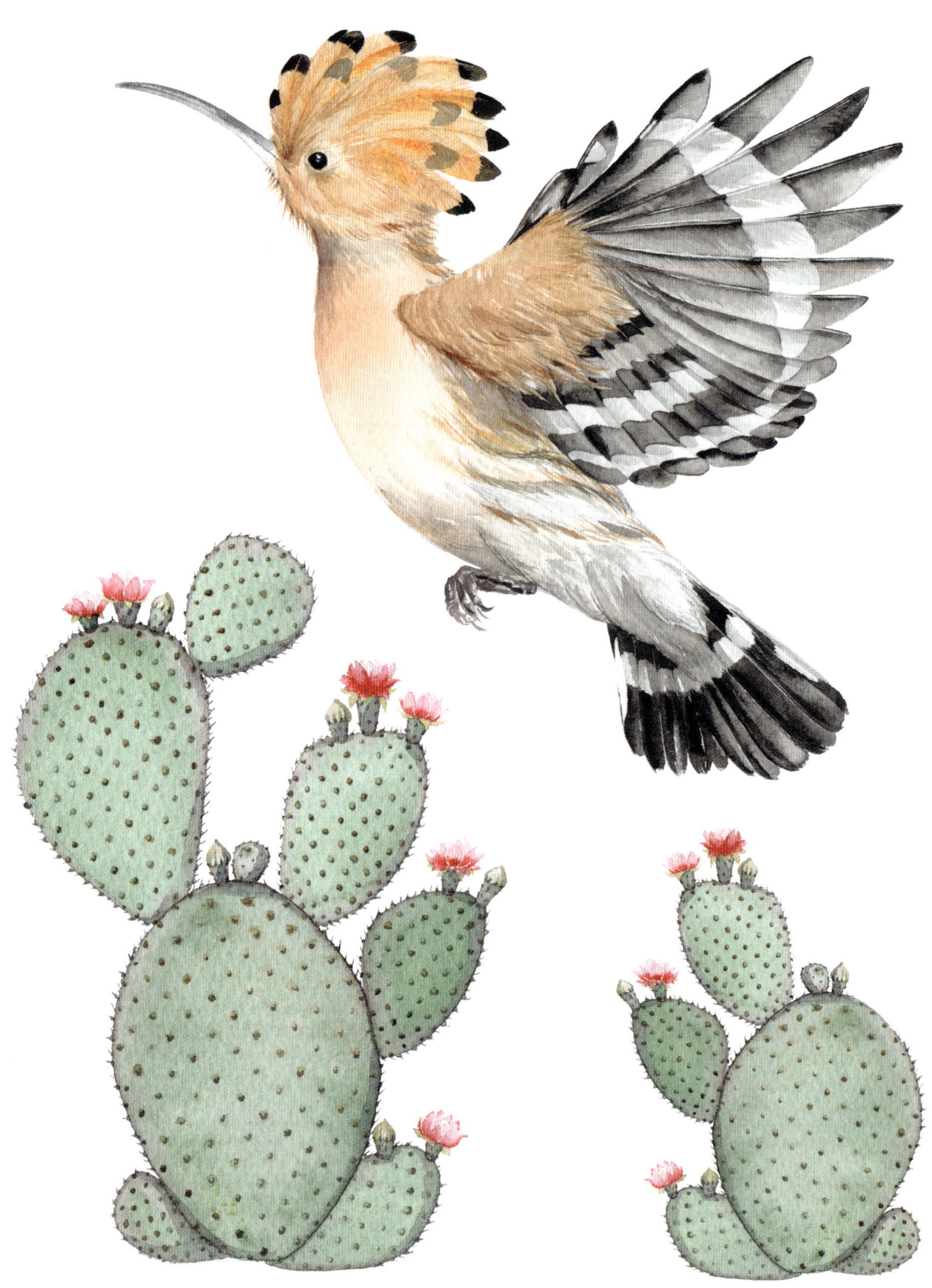

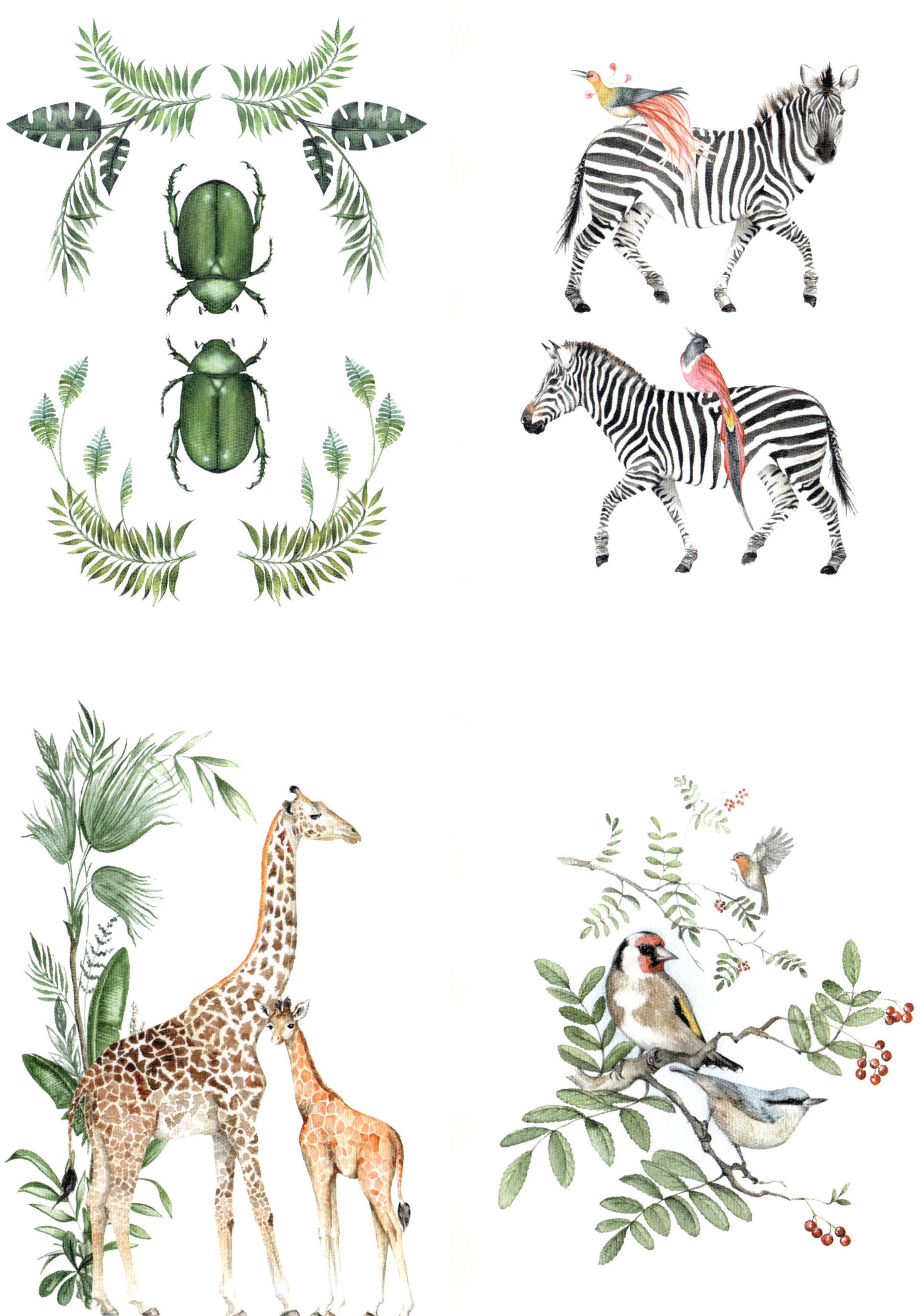

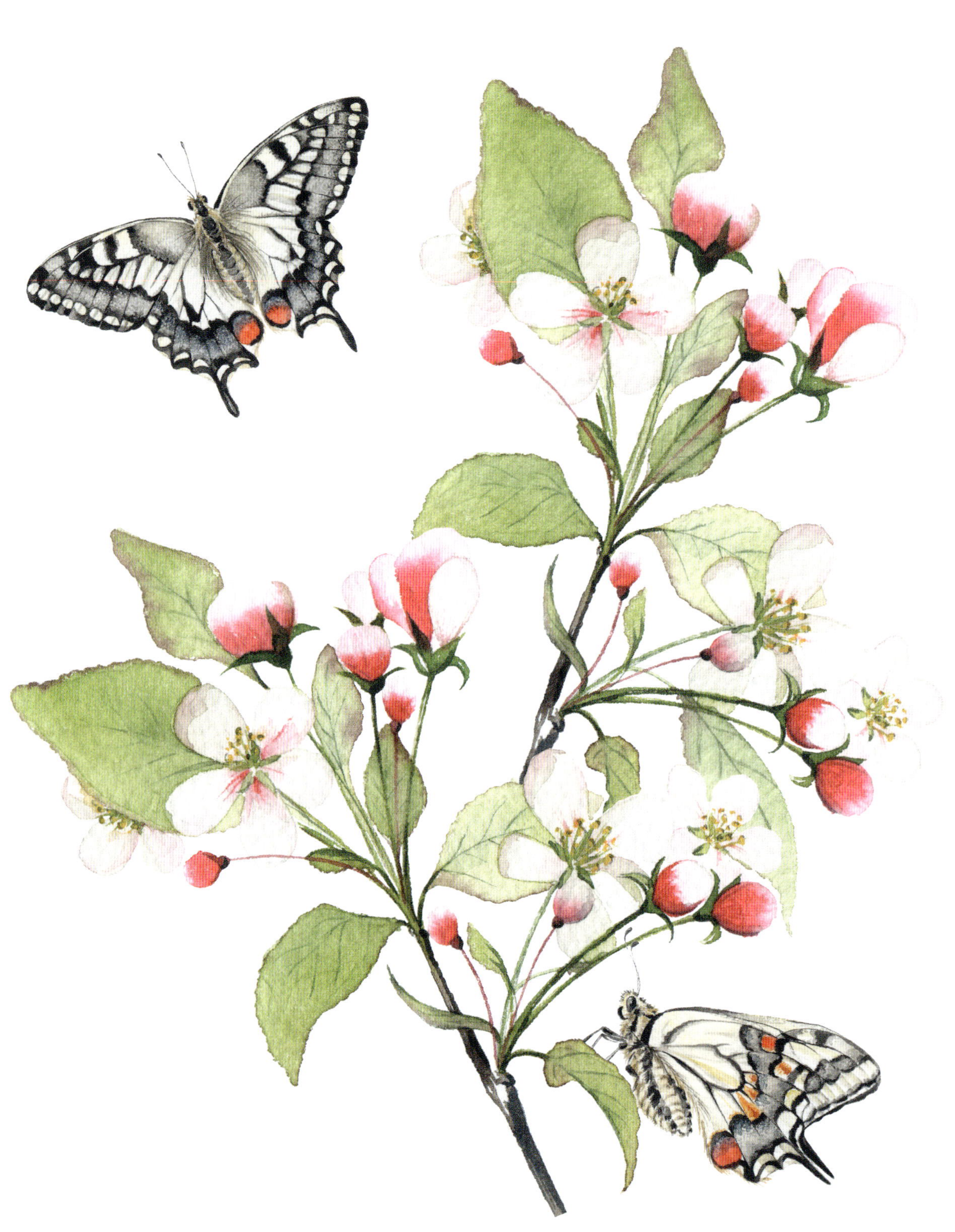

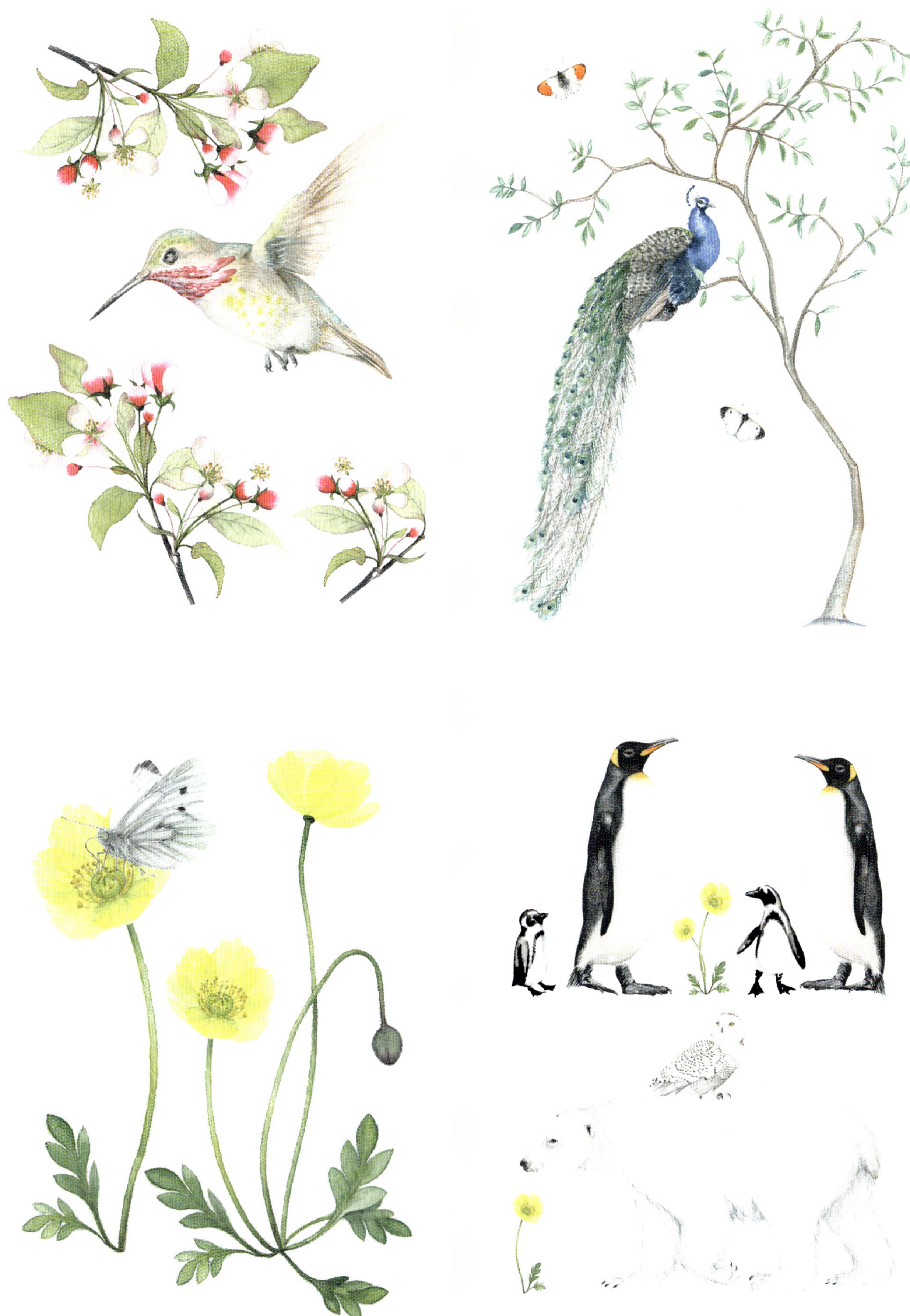

ART PAD

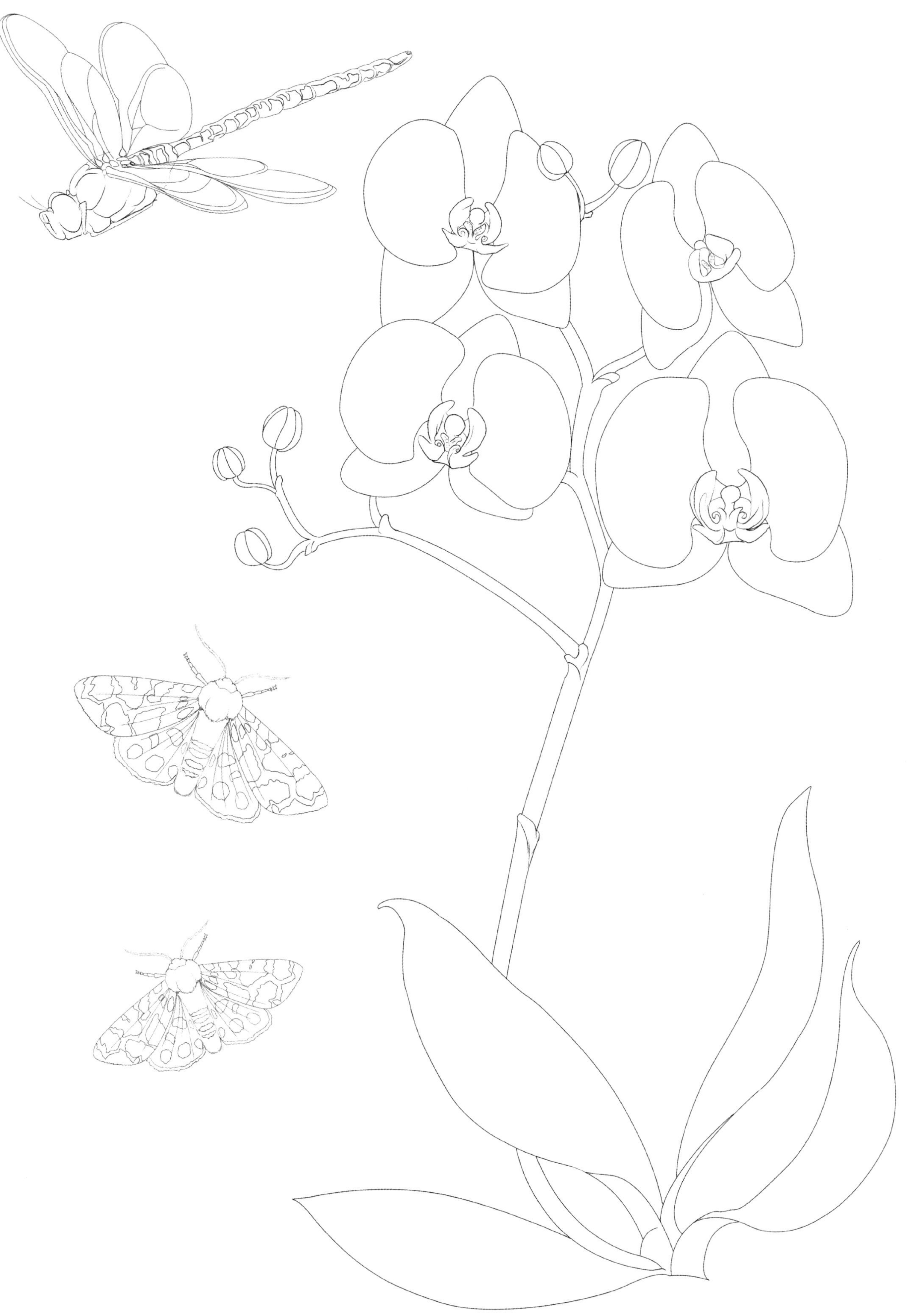

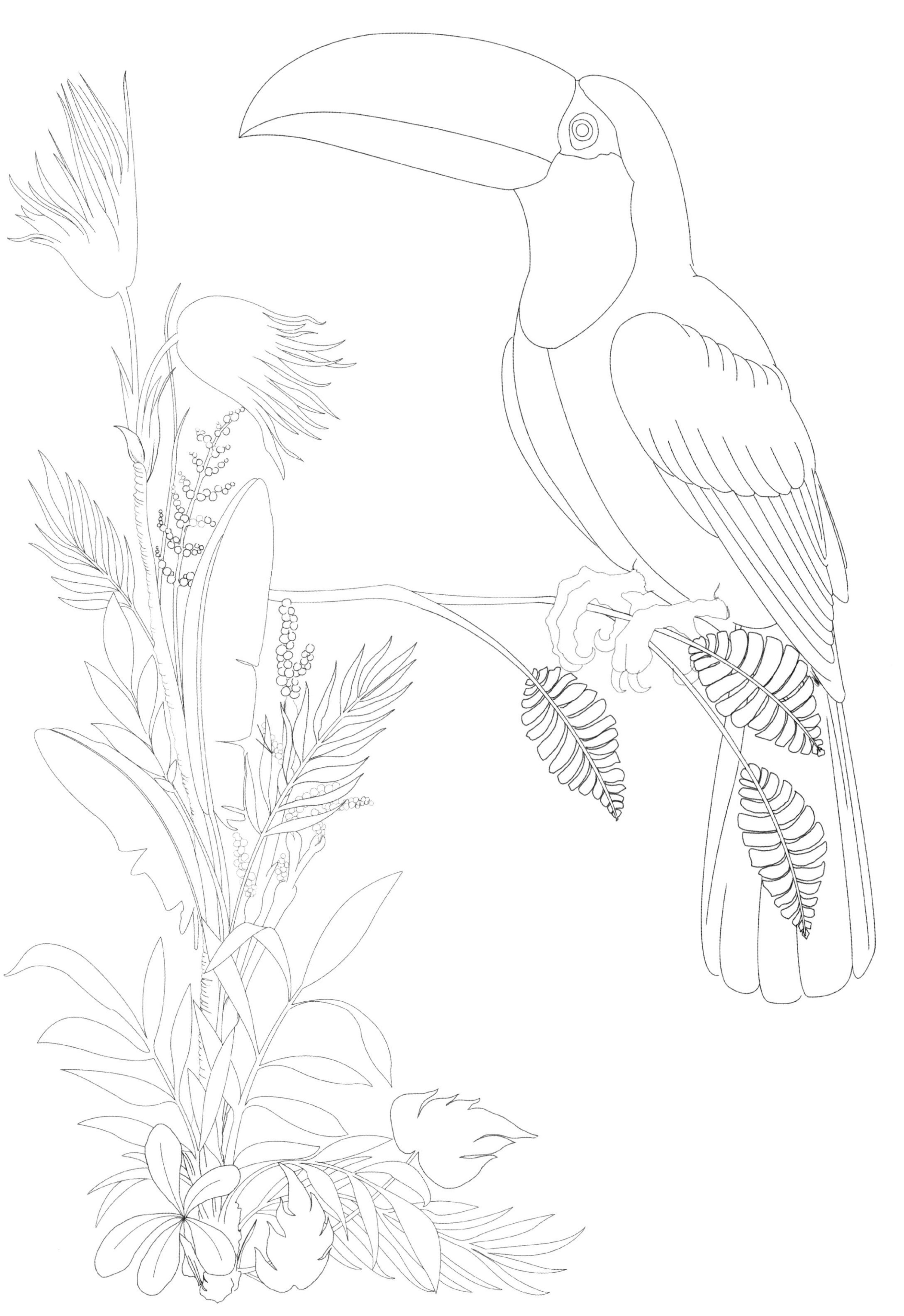

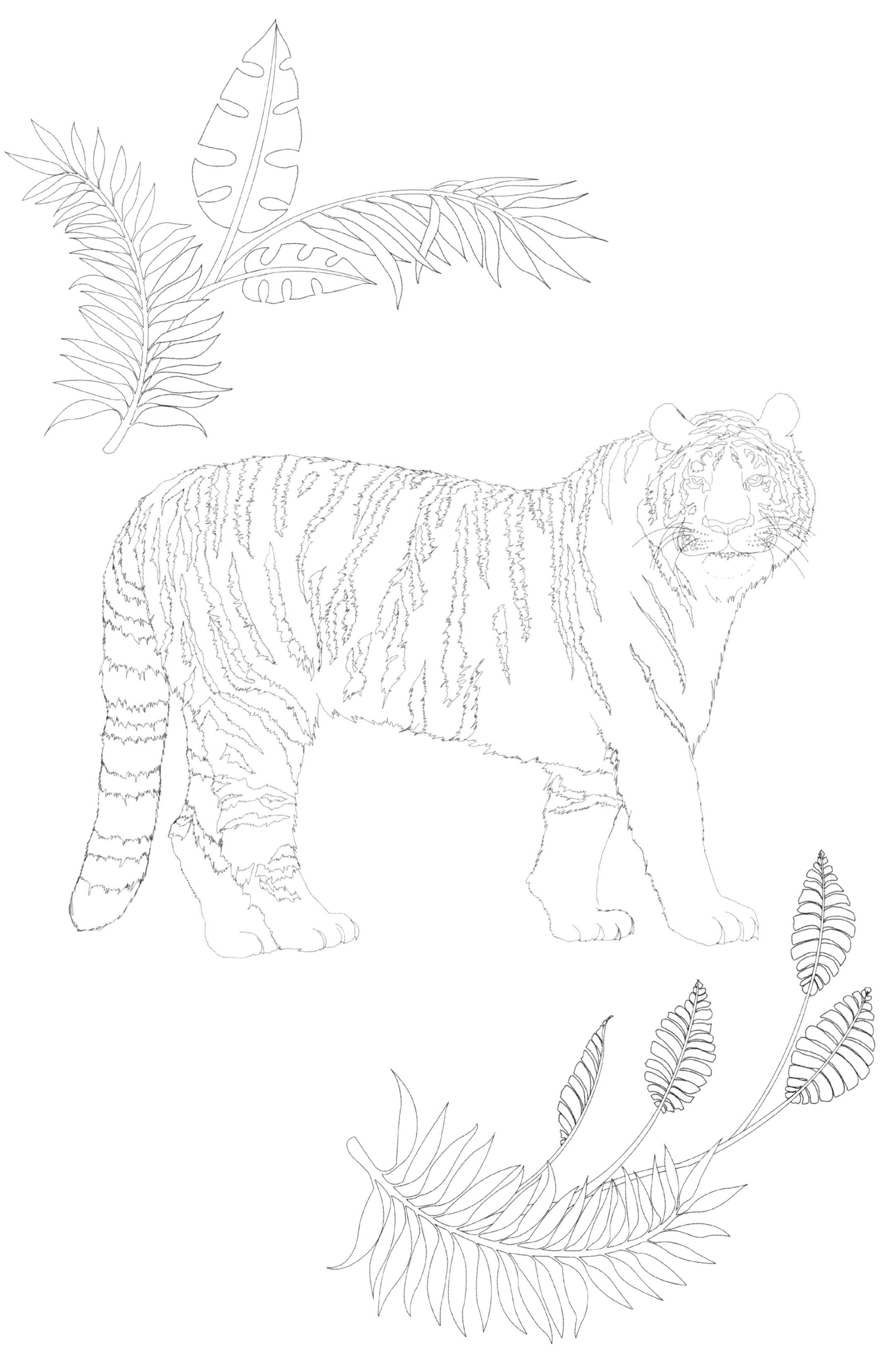

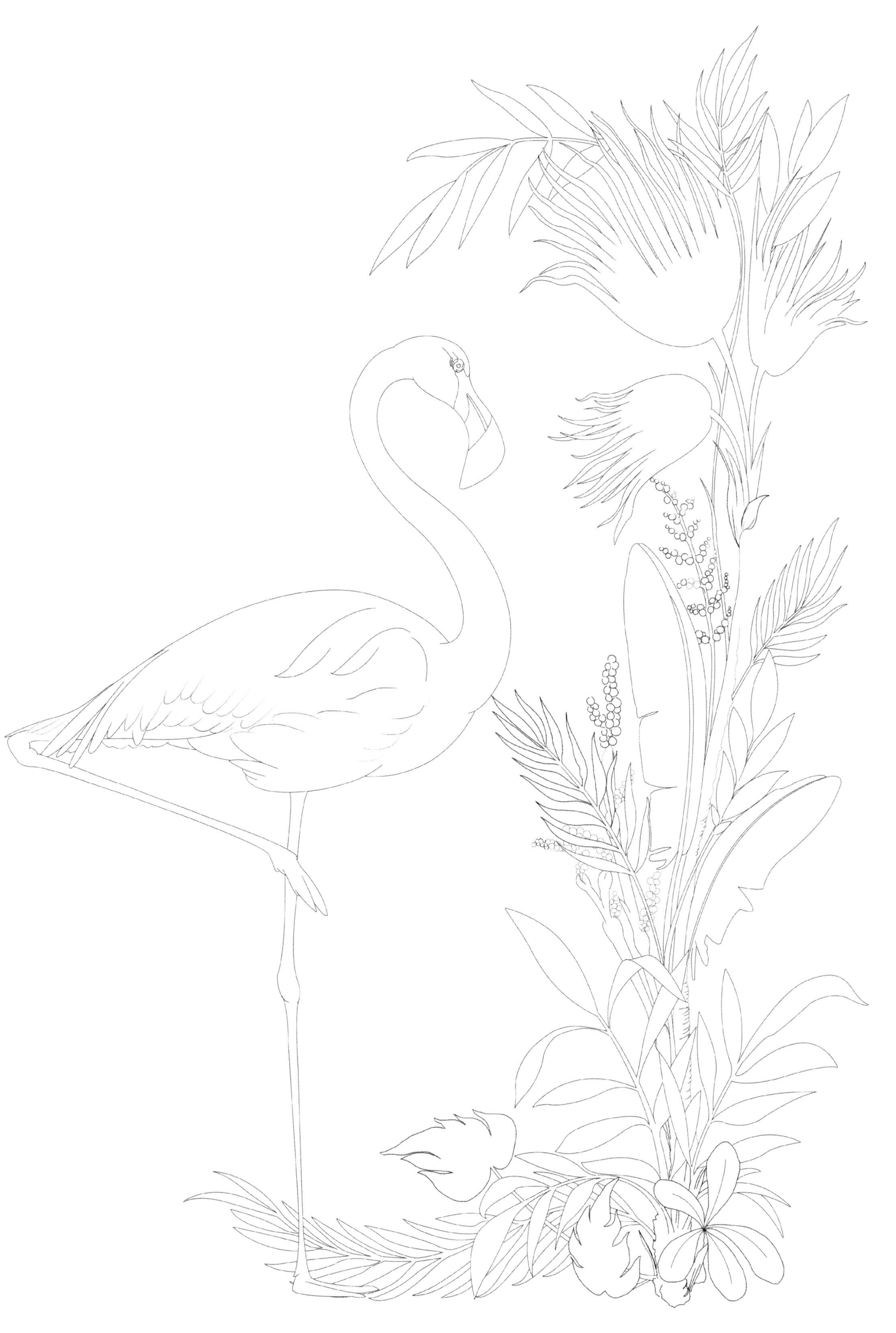

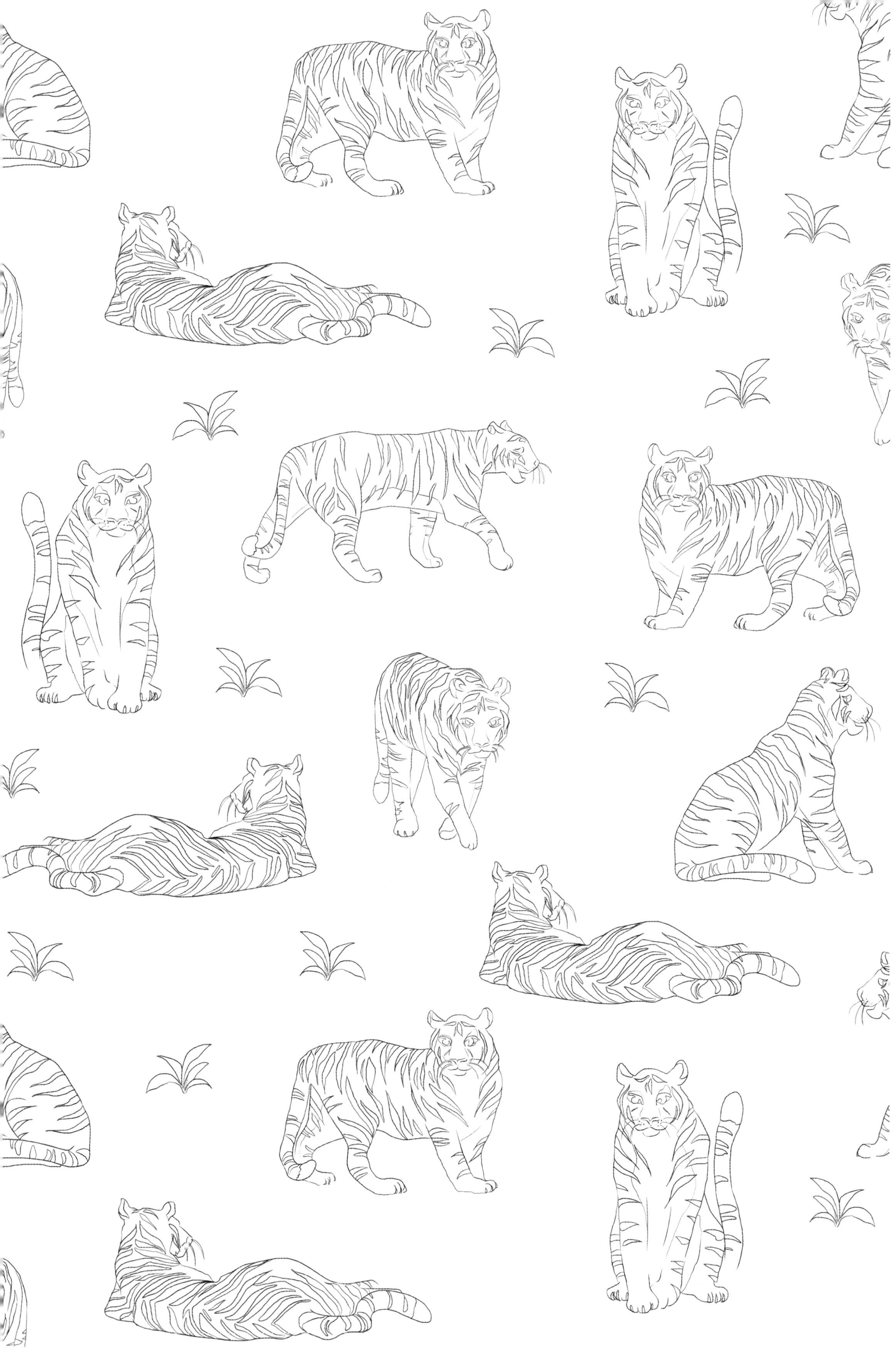

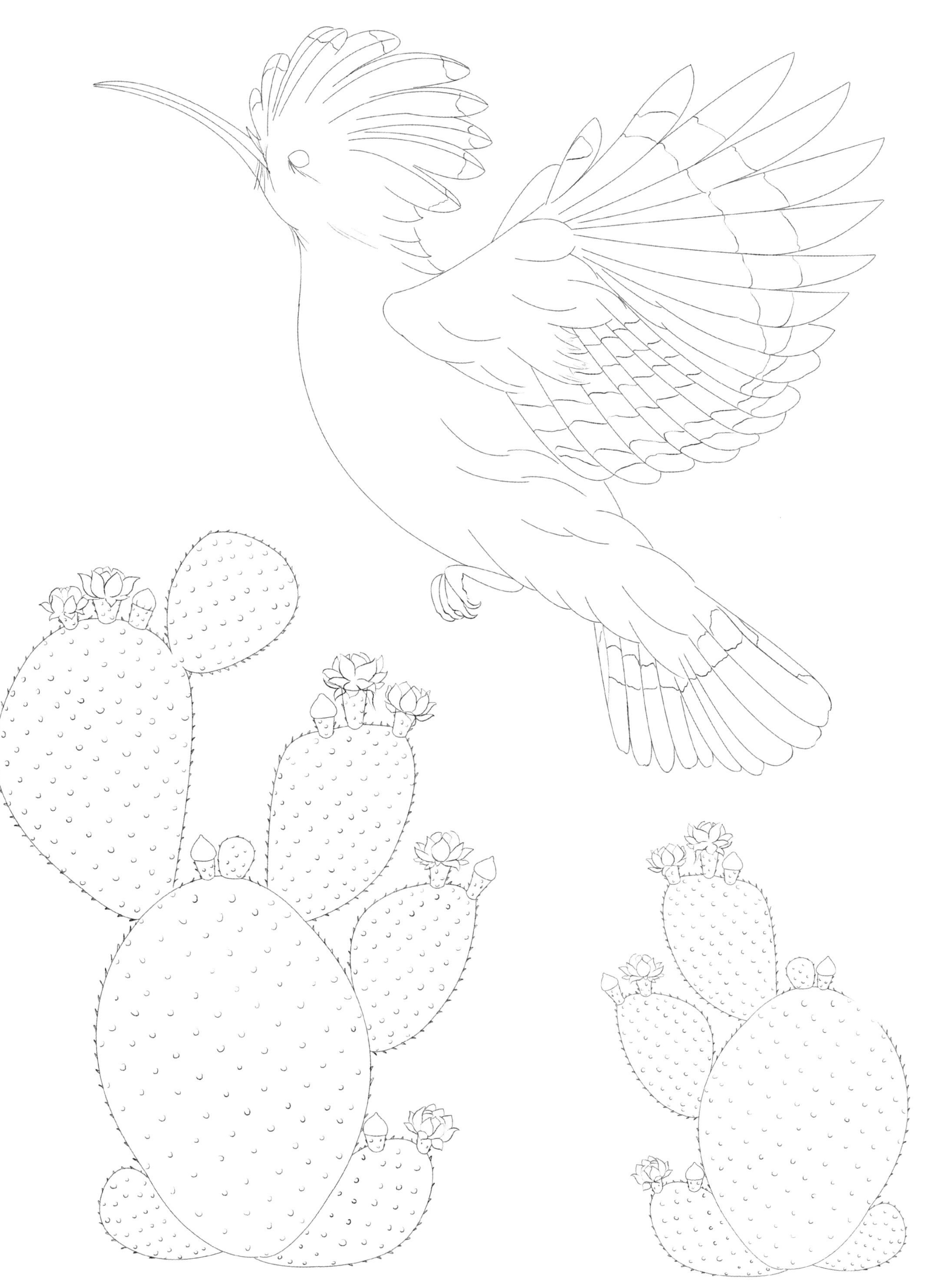

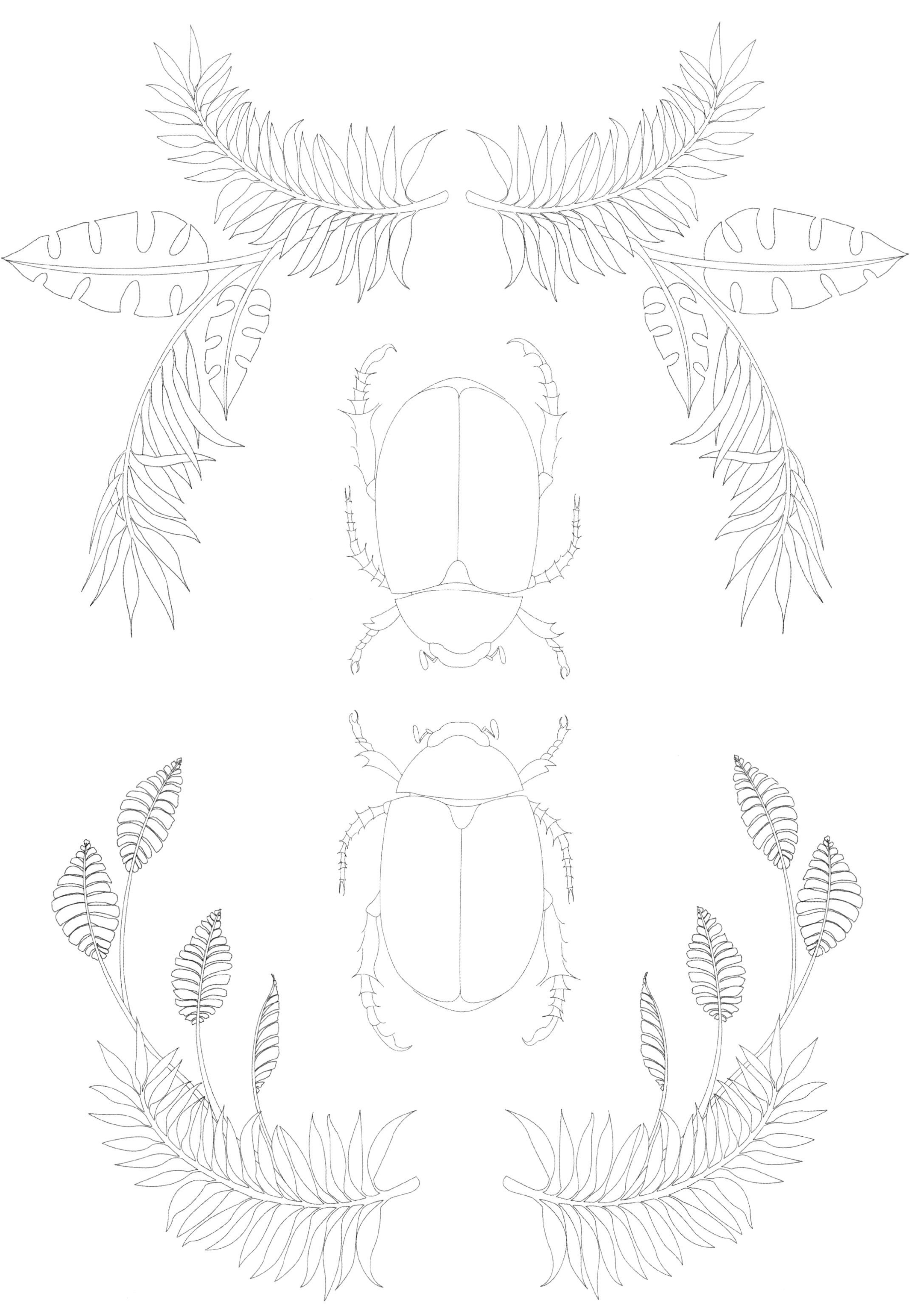

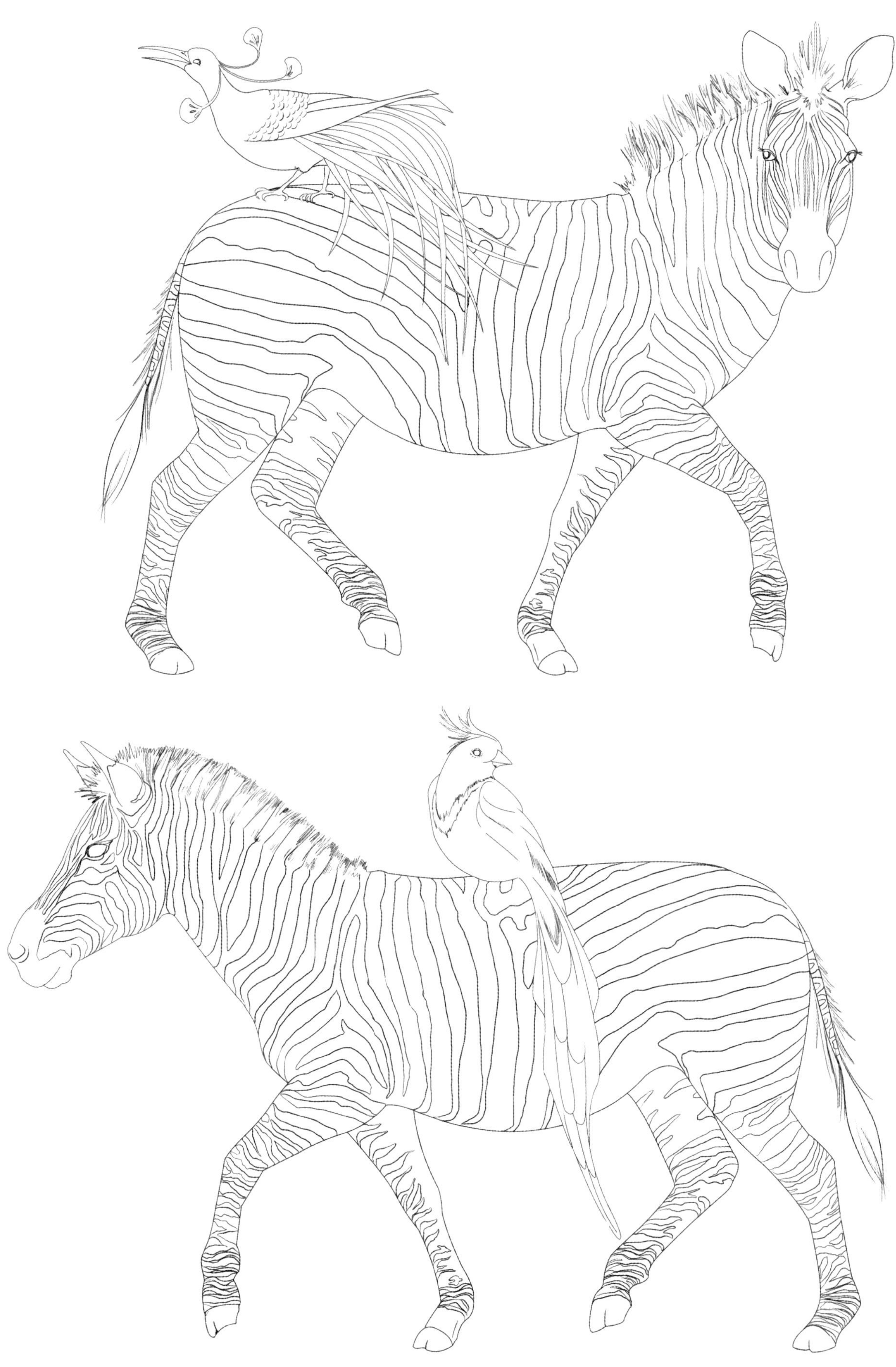

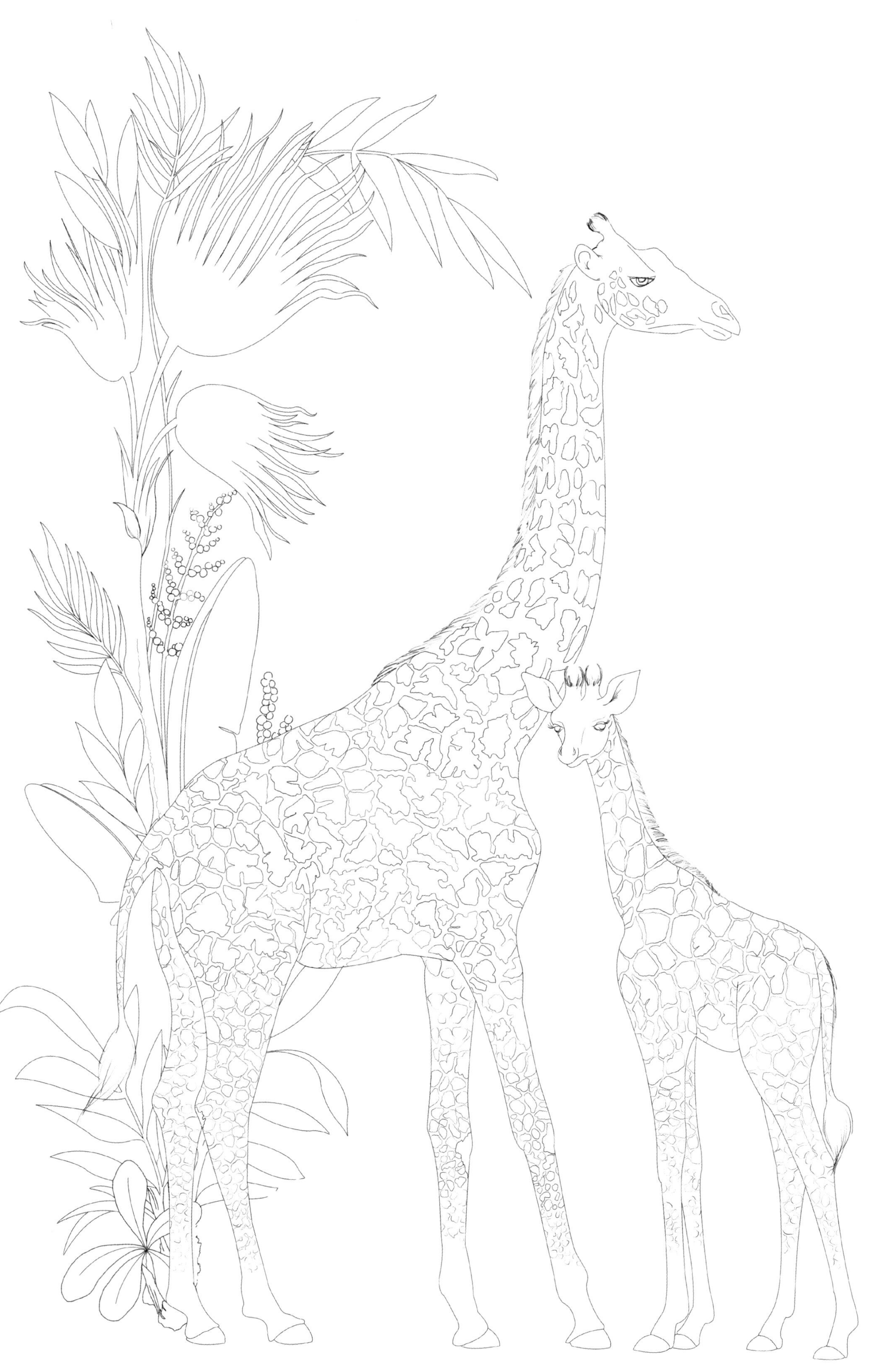

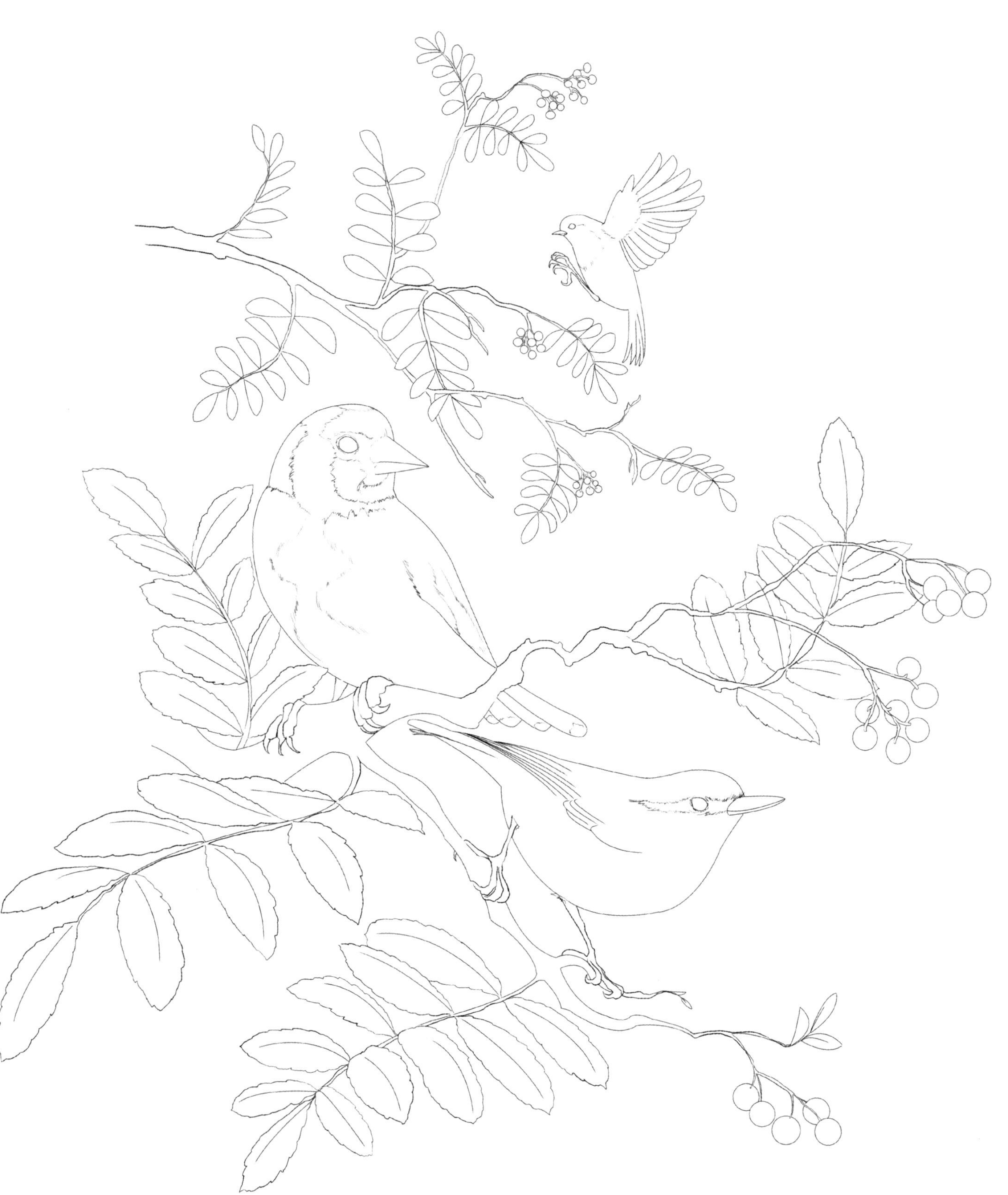

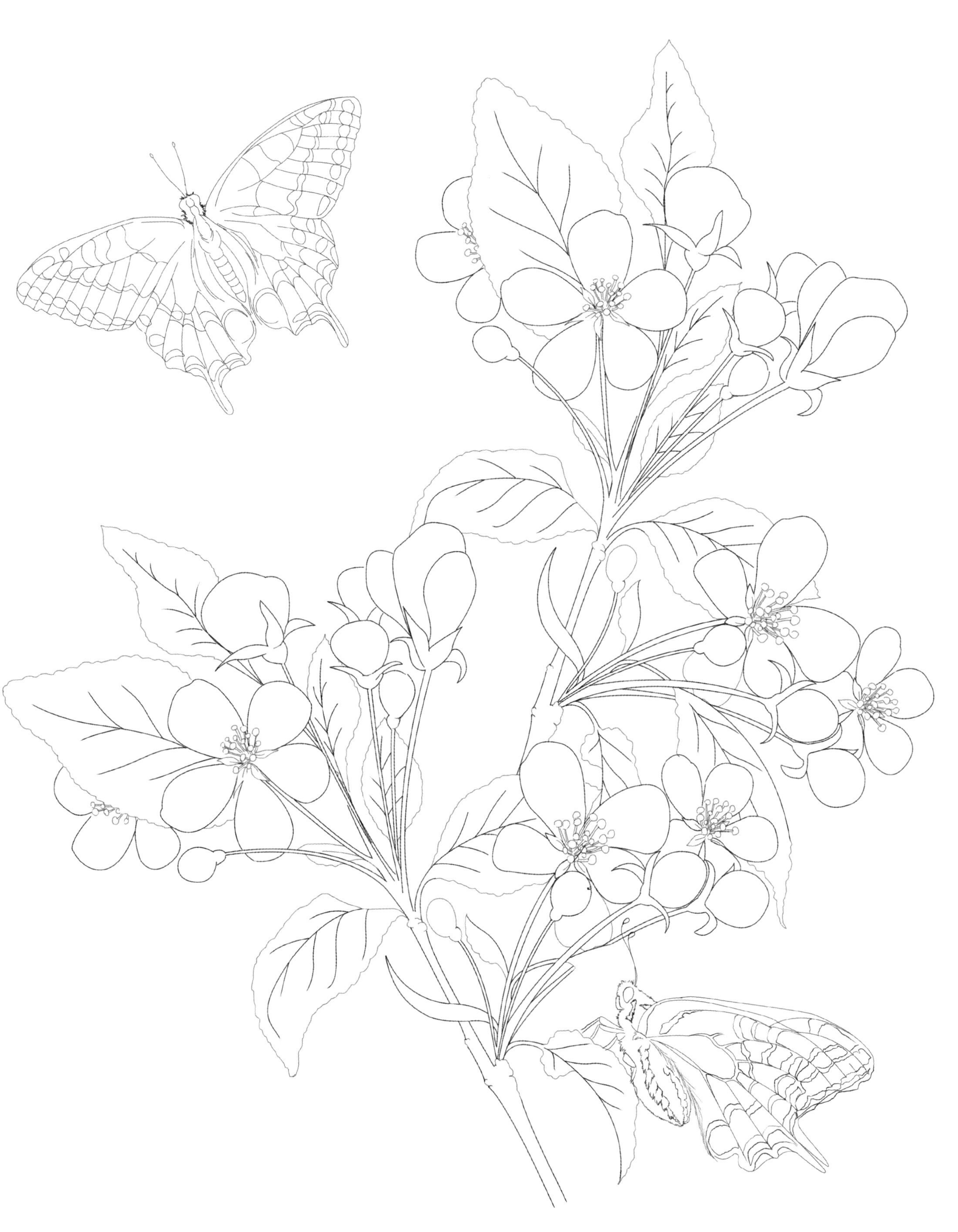

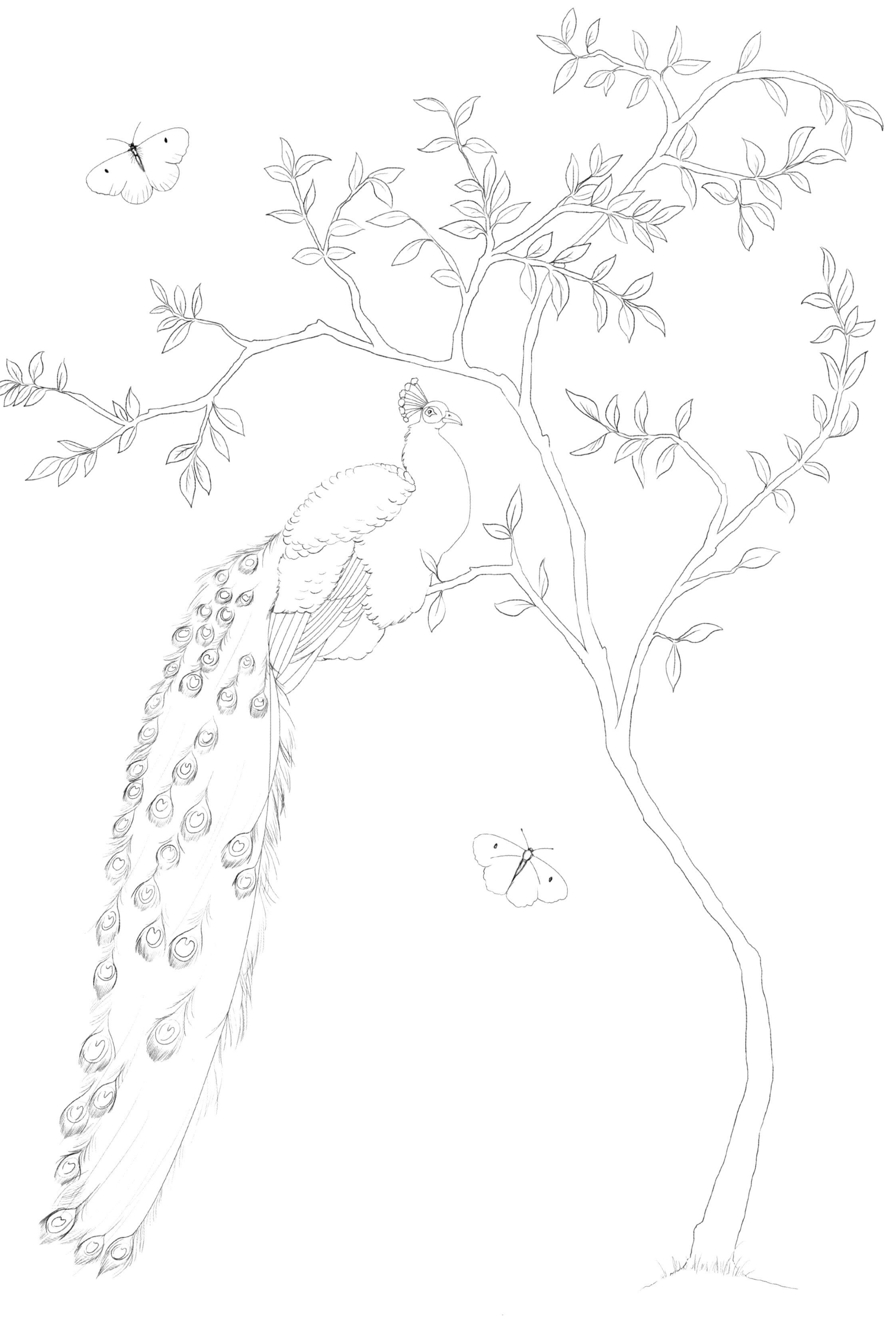

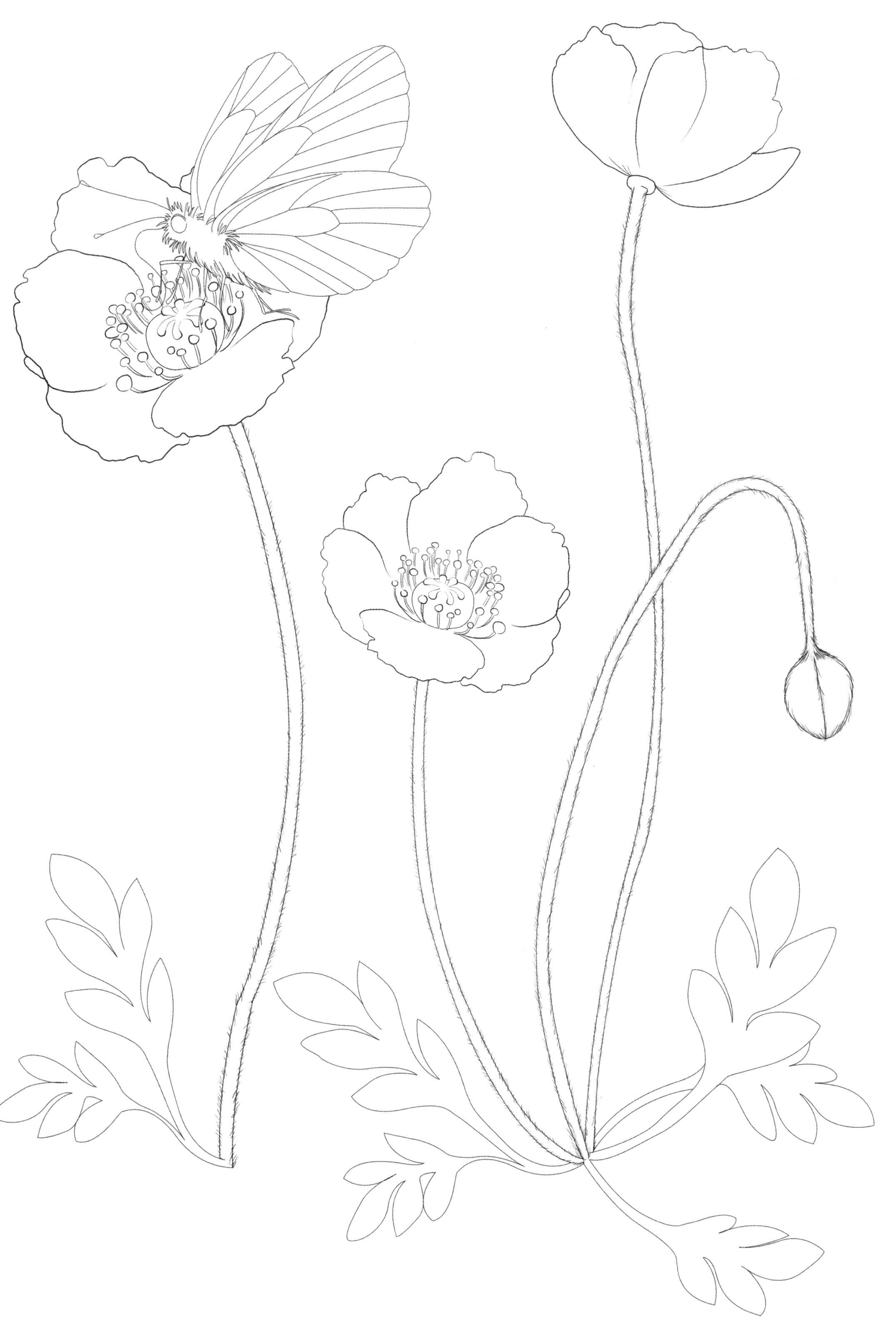

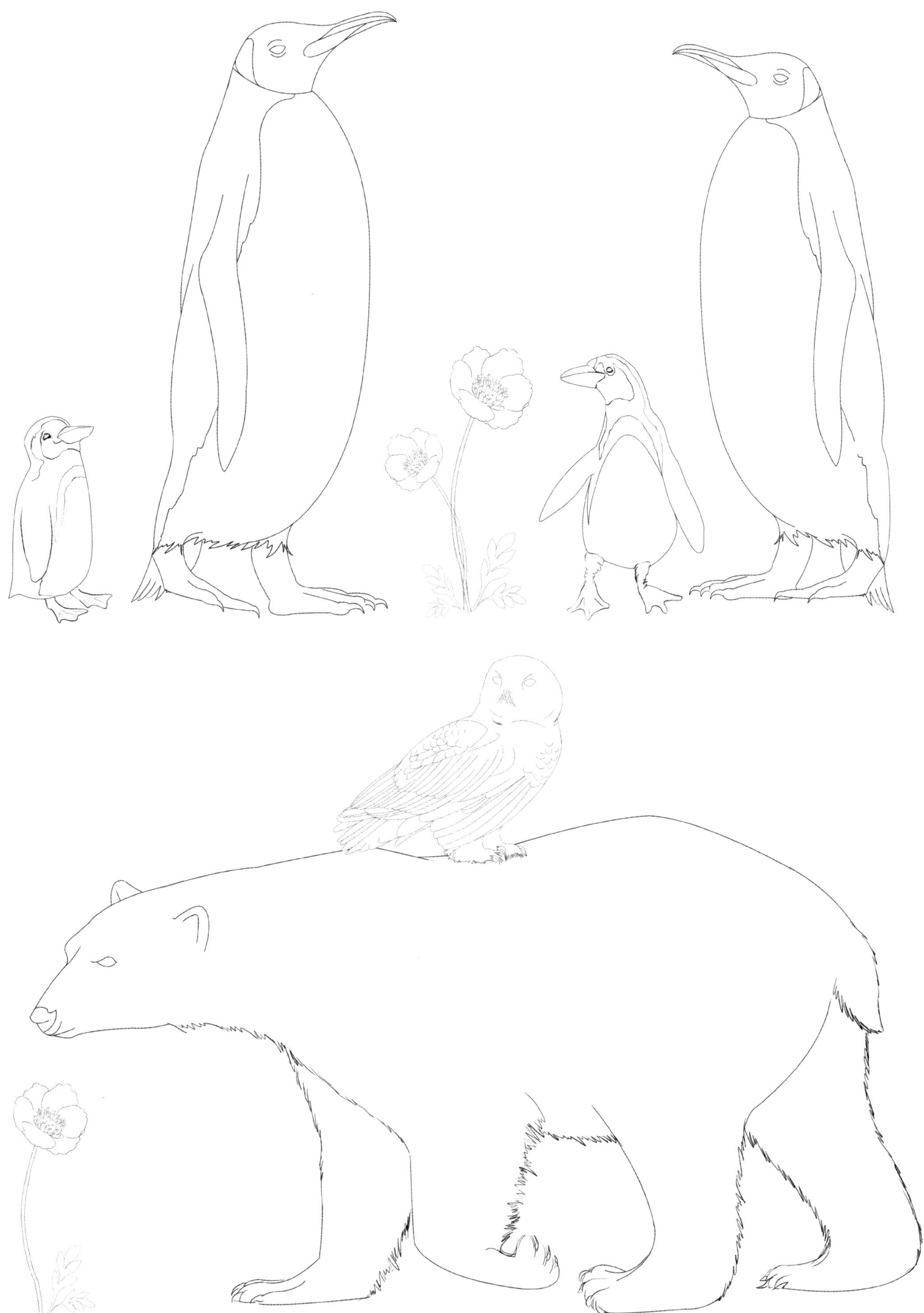